THE MAZE
UNDER THE
OLD THEATRE

A historical crime novella

ELIZABETH VON WITANOVSKI

ISBN 978-1-956696-34-9 (paperback)
ISBN 978-1-956696-35-6 (digital)

Rushmore Press LLC
1 800 460 9188
www.rushmorepress.com

Printed in the United States of America

"Acting is not a state of being . . . but a state of appearing to be."

- Noël Coward

PROLOGUE

Last floor. Jacob was ready. He didn't like Paternoster elevators. Like a metaphor of an unsettled life. The open cabins, dangerous, one above the other, moving in relentless speed allowing at best for one step out. All day long, never-ending never-stopping chain of compartments. Someone told him when he was a boy that if you missed to get out before the last floor, the cabin flipped over. It scared him for life. Jacob's leg reached high for the down coming floor. The illusion was confusing. He stepped up. Too soon! Pain in his thigh was excruciating. He had barely enough strength to stand up. Such nonsense about falling on one's head! His hand touched the side of his jacket. The gun gave him confidence. He put on the hat and walked into his meeting.

ACT I

Early 1900s, Austria

"Catch!" A little girl shot up from her child-sized blue garden chair. The light wood construction shook, the wicker weave gleaming in the full sun. She skillfully caught a little silver box before it could fall on the freshly mowed lawn.

What a pity father took her brothers fishing. She was supposedly coming down with something this morning; poor mama had to stay home with her and work on her embroidery all afternoon. The 'something' had never arrived and now they were all stuck here for the day.

She looked with excitement at the object of her desire; Marcel winked at her.

He exhaled cigarette smoke in a few short puffs to further amuse her. White bouncing rings of smoke made her laugh out loud as she charged after them to poke her little fingers through them. Her straw hat, loosely tied under her chin with a wide blue ribbon, fell on her back.

"Gerda! Behave like a young lady!" The caring voice of her mother Gloria came from underneath a vast hat brim. Her fashionable bleached straw number was the one she picked in Paris the past Spring.

"I am not a young lady!" the nine-year-old protested vehemently.

Her mother turned to their young guest. "Marcel, you shouldn't spoil her like that! A silver vesta is not suitable for little girls." There

1

was white silk chiffon and red berries arranged around the hat's round crown.

"I am not a little girl!"

"Why, of course not!" Marcel picked cherries from the crystal glass bowl sitting on one of three small, round side tables. Dressed in white crisp damask, they were the comfortable height for those lounging around throughout long, lazy summer. His index finger issued an invitation; it was obeyed immediately. Gerda stepped towards his chair and smiled.

Marcel chose a pair of cherries "Turn."

His suntanned fingers started arranging them around her delicate petite ears.

"You are not a little girl. You are. . ." he chose one more pair, took Gerda's shoulders, and turned her like a doll to her other profile. ". . . the future Baroness Van Getz!"

She grinned and started fidgeting. His hand had to hold her head still.

He evaluated his *chef d'oeuvre* with a short whistle. Gerda laughed and touched her "earrings."

"I'll have them made for you in gold and diamonds one day, like the Russian tzarinas' wedding jewels." He handed her more cherries to eat.

"Now, really, Marcel." A gust of wind tried to steal Gloria's hat. It pulled painfully on her light brown hair.

"Ah!" She hated that pinch. She tossed the embroidery attached on a wooden ring on the other white wicker chair next to her. Her nanny would pull on her hair like that when she failed to follow exactly her orders. Gloria made a huge fuss when choosing a nanny for her precious little girl. Her hand in the short white crochet summer glove, she unfastened her hair pins. She fixed the hat firmly over her hair. "Why do you tease that child like that?"

"I am not teasing!" Marcel picked the round, slippery stone from his mouth and pinched it; his shot went straight into Gerda's direction.

"I am not a child!" said Gerda with her mouth full. She tried to return the attack.

"You both are," whispered Gerda's mother into the laces of her low white décolleté. She was trying to fix her long hairpins. The tip of her tongue reached the middle of her upper lip for support. A taste of cherries from Marcel's stolen kiss was still there.

Marcel winked at Gerda again. He made it clear that they were accomplices. She blushed. By now, her white organza apron with a big bow in the back was filled with deep pink spots. Her mother noticed.

"Mademoiselle!" called Gloria to the governess. "Would you take this soiled sugar plum fairy home and change her to something clean for dinner?"

That evening, after her mother's goodnight kisses, Gerda waited for her governess to turn off the light; she listened and snuck out of bed. The house was silent. She reached under her pillow. Marcel's silver match box—the vesta—was there, cool and smooth.

Gerda crossed the polished geometric pattern of the parquet floor on the tiptoes of her bare feet. Between the small side table and the large white and blue flowerpot in the corner her heel pushed one of the parquets. It slid horizontally underneath the flooring with a barely audible click.

A small, shallow hiding space revealed itself. It was just big enough for a little treasure box. Gerda discovered it by chance only last year.

Inside a tin that she had placed there were small objects—interesting stones from her walks with Marcel, postcards signed by him, and an identical silver vesta just like the one she was holding in her palm. She took it from Marcel's pocket during one of his visits to have a little piece of him. She forgave herself for it immediately. She promised it was just a loan. What a beautiful little object!

Now she had two. They were engraved with Marcel's cipher. The interior shone with gold. Its silver body was decorated with fine engravings of laurel leaves; they continued from the side to the top of the narrow lid. The rough match-strike ribbon was on its side as part of an ornament. Such a sweet little trinket! Gerda was standing there, hesitant. Her bare feet had traded their temperature with the parquets. The little foot slowly closed the secret hideaway.

The new small present was lovingly placed back under Gerda's pillow.

She narrowed her eyes. Through her many eyelashes, she pictured the letter M framed by laurel wreath in the pointed male shape of Marcel's coat of arms. Her sleepy mind played with the image; the cipher changed to an interlocked M&G. Gerda gave a sigh of relief and closed her eyes. Now she knew for certain that one day, when she grows up, she would become Gerda—Baroness Van Getz.

"You shouldn't be talking to my little girl like that," Gerda's mother said late that night. She took a cigarette from Marcel's soft mouth, took a draft, and exhaled.

"She takes everything so seriously." Her fingertips tried to rid her tongue of excess tobacco. Marcel kissed her naked navel, glossy from sweat, and took back his cigarette. "But I am serious. If I can't marry you, I will . . ."

"Had I not known you for so long . . ."—she took her cigarette from him—" . . . I'd have you whipped out of my house!" She laughed and slowly merged into the pillows behind her. Her arm stretched, holding the lit cigarette off the bed.

Marcel's hand followed its full length. Her body slid under him. She started kissing his chest; her mouth was indulging in salty drops of sweat, still there, holding onto his skin and his dark curls, intoxicating in their abundance. His excited fingers took the cigarette from hers and placed it by the bronze base of the French table lamp.

The hiding device sprung open. The click echoed throughout Gloria's empty bedroom. She didn't feel tired. The dawn tinted the outdoors in hues of grays and blues. She didn't notice. The slim drawer slid out. There was nothing to give that safe spot away. It looked like one of many inlaid ornaments; twists, arabesques, and meanders—all designed to trick your eyes. Gloria took out all the little notes she'd received from Marcel over the last few years:

"I have to kiss you now!"

"I have to kiss you under the old oak."

"I have to have you."

Different pieces of paper, different times of day, different locations—Marcel's unmistakable handwriting, his favorite phrase, unchanged.

Gloria looked straight into her looking glass—an aging woman, past her prime. Her oldest will be thirty next autumn; the youngest . . . she's growing too fast. Gloria moved her chin up looking for a more forgiving angle, then one more slow movement down.

"Liar!" she whispered to her reflection.

She swept the notes, now spread disorderly on the narrow desktop, into a small pile. Her palms were cold. They stopped trembling by the time she crossed to the tall white-tile stove. The fire was crackling inside them.

Gloria dropped the hem of her silk nightgown from her pinch to reach for the shiny brass knob of the upper of the two small doors. The heat grabbed her face. Her skin felt as if it had shrunk. She didn't budge. She didn't feel a thing.

Decisively, she stepped closer. Her hand, with Marcel's love notes, shot above the flames. She dropped them all in. The effect of the warm, flickering light made her features look smooth, and blissfully young.

Gerda's parents never asked Marcel, the young baron Van Getz, to be their guest ever again.

"Why do I have to explain that again?' Bruno Gottlieb looked at the group of chorus girls. "Are you deaf?"

His was one of the best theatres in Vienna. He had been always adamant to keep it that way. Now this! What a month this was! One of the tenors broke his ankle; the young ingenue didn't wait and got herself pregnant! All of that now just when he started rehearsing the new show.

"Take it from the top," he commanded them, tired and irritated.

He nodded to the pianist, "Start from the lalalala."

Sitting behind his upright piano, facing the stage, Hubert Schweiger was a keen helper in this operetta house. Bruno Gottlieb was his old friend. They studied music together at the Viennese Conservatory.

Bruno wanted to be an actor. He had more talent for business. Hubert had only one talent. He could play anything he touched—except for women. He just loved to watch them. Some of the girls would tease him mercilessly about it. Usually those who weren't shy to "thank" their directors and leading men behind the paravane in their dressing-room.

It was known that Bruno had never expected anything like that. There wasn't the proverbial director's couch in his theatre. Surrounded by half naked bodies all day long, it was not the flesh he was after. And that was rare to find.

"Thank you, all, for today!" Bruno had enough. His patience expired an hour ago; his perseverance held him here. He didn't swear. He would save his peppery swear words for the next rehearsal. He was never truly vulgar nor dirty; his were words of impatience with a pinch of humor.

Someone opened the door to the atrium. Wind flashed through, sending the fragrance of fresh grass in the dark space. "Such nuisance!" It wasn't clear if he meant his situation or the rain that was pouring since last night. He walked to the piano. He was tired and depressed. "What am I going to do, Hubert?"

"An audition, what else? That's what you have to do—and *Presto.*"

He was right. It had to be done quickly. Bruno could always rely on him for a friendly push. He reached in his pocket for the cigarette. His cigarette case was empty. This was another annoying mishap of today. "I'll be in my office."

Hubert closed the music score. "I think I'll go to have something to eat." He left the book on the piano. The stage manager will take care of it. He caught a glimpse of the men's dresser, crossing the stage in front of the black backdrop. He was in a hurry. Hubert needed to talk to him; the man was a skillful tailor. Hubert needed a new pair of pants. Franz had his moments though. It started after he returned from the Great War; he used to be more reliable. Still, no suits fit like the ones made by Franz Hirsch.

Hubert checked his watch. It was almost five hours to the beginning of the performance. He could surely have a bite and coffee. He started walking towards the shortcut, the passage through the underground.

Hubert was fascinated by his new pair of shoes. He was walking without making any noise! They were from his sister, from America. He always wished for them; she sent him two pairs for his birthday. They had their soles made of rubber, so quiet that you could walk across the stage unheard! She wrote that people started calling them "sneakers."

Bruno Gottlieb crossed the stage and turned into the short hallway. The door of his office was never locked. He sat down heavily at his oakwood desk. The light-colored wood made it always look as if there was a spotlight on it. It didn't cheer him up today. He was worried.

When he decided to buy this theatre, it was in disorder. Not a ruin yet, but close. It stood in a shallow spot not far from the river. The last hundred-year flood ruined the cellars and soaked the stage. It all seemed beyond repair. In the fifty years since the floodwater dried out, the city built a new high embankment. The property of the Old Theatre was suddenly surrounded by high grounds on all four sides. Luckily, the structure, the granite stones, and the mortar were intact. All his engineers agreed. Bruno closed the deal.

It was only that old logic of his, and some superstition, that made him rebuild on top.

Not to disturb the blueprint, not to erase old Genius Loci; not to scare any of the Muses away. The new stage over the old one; the new backstage over the original structure.

Bruno even had a small atrium garden built for his actors. To go out in between the acts, or after a matinee; to sit on the garden bench, breathe, enjoy the greenery.

It wasn't until the new building was almost complete when he found out about the murder. They all kept that story hush hush__A famous actress from the Bernini theatre clan was murdered there. She was found stabbed in her dressing room.

That part was now in the underground—"the Maze," as it was nicknamed.

Great storage. Exactly what this theatre needs.

And the passage? Great idea! It was his business stroke of genius, Hubert says, to buy that one-story house across the street. Bruno felt old satisfaction returning. The small cafe quickly gained quite a following. He was a good businessman; he was a good theatre director.

Bruno stood up and replaced the smoking-box. No time for pleasure.

"Miss Schlegel!"

A small pince-nez on her fragile long nose, making large brown eyes appear smudged, her honest face emerged in the doorframe. "Yes, Mr. Gottlieb?"

"We have an audition to announce."

On a rainy day like this, the passage was unbeatable. Hubert walked down the winding staircase to the underground. It was the genius of Bruno. The large storage space, the Maze, opened on one side under the stairs. There, the passage started as a long hallway ending in another staircase on the other side. Those stairs took you up to a gateway connecting the main house, where the cafe was, to the back building with a courtyard.

Hubert heard a muffled conversation somewhere down in front of him. The narrow-slanted windows above could barely help to navigate the stairs. The light bulbs down here were scarce. With others down here now, Hubert's tendency to jog through this shadowy space seemed like a silly idea. His thoughts down here had always turned to that murdered actress. Where was that spot? He should ask . . . or not. Hubert turned the corner__and froze.

The two men who didn't hear him coming turned to stone blocks. They chose the spot exactly to be able to hear well ahead if anybody was coming. Their faces were two exclamation marks, like the painting of a scream Hubert saw in a gallery last week.

One of the men was just about to take a tiny lick of a white powder from his finger. The other one was holding a little box for him. *Cocaine!* flashed in Hubert's mind and then he recognized_ Franz!

Two pairs of petrified hands were waiting, suspended in the air. Hubert held his breath, his stomach pulled in and up like when he's ready to wave his baton.

The stranger suddenly reached inside his breast pocket. Hubert didn't wait; his body darted forward to sprint. The two men saw the danger right away; they needed to silence him.

Hubert had never run this fast; he never ran for his life. A muffled shot banged around his ears. Hubert knew this was not a long passage. Maybe someone will appear from the opposite side. His strokes were as long as his legs allowed. His silent run was followed by heavy hits of two pairs of leather soles. His legs started to hurt. He was not an athlete. He tried to focus. The stairs on the other side of the passage came to view. His willpower was pushing him forward; another shot rang around his body. He knew they would not dare once he was close to the cafe. Hubert felt his strength wearing down fast. Finally, the stairs! He was safe!

He took two steps at a time, flew to the gateway, and then he saw his way out—the courtyard. Poles with lines of wet laundry hanging dead down soaked anew in the rain. Curtains to hide behind, to run away through the back gate. Hubert dashed in that direction.

A shot slapped the wet sheets. It burnt holes in several of them. The bullet flew through, shiny, without principles, killing Hubert Schweiger—the musician—instantly.

This was not the first time during her schooling here that Helena was called to the principal's office. After a decade, when the previous headmistress stepped down, Miss Honfleur was offered the position. The vote was almost unanimous. Only one voice hesitated: "Perhaps, too dramatic for such an important post."

The door to her office was dark, tall, divided into two sections; from the distance, it looked like an exclamation mark. Behind them, the practically full-circle office—called "The Watchtower" by generations of young women—had windows all around. You could see the Alps wherever you looked.

This was what Helena liked the best about being in school here in Switzerland —mountains and lakes. Being called Helli was what Helena disliked with passion. Her nickname was propagated by teachers who saw her potential. In their opinion, it was suggestive of a light, floating spirit; her artistic streak that ran through everything this young woman touched was self-evident.

The door opened with a muffled sound. It swept the Turkish carpet in all available hues of blue and orange leaving the trace of a wedge. Helena, a petite dark-blond girl, stepped in.

She was the daughter of a wealthy family that lived somewhere— Miss Honfleur suddenly couldn't recall—in Surrey, the garden of England, or was it Kent? Her brush with guilt made her stand up.

She had never stood up for anyone. Helena's heart sank. This must be serious. There they were, face-to-face. Unlike their past encounters, this was not their battlefield today.

"Please, do sit, Helli."

Helli? Helena knew immediately that, whatever it was, it was worse than she could have ever imagined. She hated that nickname as much as she despised her name, Helena. Helena, the Beautiful. How many times did she have to live through that tease about the Trojan War? Her newest, most exciting plan was to change her name to Helga the first possible chance she had!

"It's your parents, dear."

There was silence.

"Your parents, Helli . . . they . . . they are . . . gone." There was a pause in which the headmistress kept closely observing the young woman. She was looking carefully into the symmetrical face, but she wasn't able to detect any emotion.

The headmistress started feeling much more uneasy than if she had witnessed Helena's loud, hysterical breakdown.

This perturbing silence was not what was supposed to be happening in her scenario. Her speech jolted back in a swift allegro. It came out as one uninterrupted word, one tone, one breath. "I am so sorry, dear child nothing could have been done an avalanche last week—they went to St. Moritz to ski, as you know, and . . ." She had exhausted all of her oxygen and had to sit down.

But Helena did not know. She knew nothing about her parents' life. They kept forgetting to inform Helena, the only child they had and ever wanted, about their moves around the globe. They were devoted only to each other. They had her, Helena, because her mother wanted to experience pregnancy with the man she'd adored. Once the little girl was born, there were nannies, and then, as soon as possible, little Helena was shipped to France to a boarding school. She was three years old then.

Helena stood there in silence. She felt enormously relieved. She had no idea what it was she'd expected to be the horrid news, but this was not it. Helena pulled the chair towards herself. She couldn't remain standing up any longer.

Finally! That was precisely how the headmistress had pictured it. That was also how she wished to speak about that scene at the next school-board meeting, "And then, that poor girl . . . suddenly an orphan . . ."

The hike up the steep slope, which Helena took yesterday afternoon, almost broke her legs. She sat down heavily with a thump.

Madame Honfleur closed her eyes, and a faint agreeable smile changed the thin line of her mouth; now, she was able to finish her story in front of the school board the only way it had to be done:

". . . under the weight of the horrid news, Helena—our poor girl, our dear, dear Helli, the tragic orphan—sat down and. . ." With a sniff the headmistress covered her face with a white handkerchief and sobbed.

The Austrian state of Vienna, 1920s

The restaurant was full. Crowded, noisy with thin clouds of smoke, like cobwebs hanging midair wall to wall. Smelling traditionally of goulash, sauerkraut, and wine, it was a popular dig for artists from all walks of life. When the loud group of Viennese actors entered one of the restaurant's four spaces created by arches dated back to Roman times, tables were already pushed together all along the wall. Weak yellow bulbs brightened up the white walls behind the long wooden benches.

Everybody had found their place. Helga was the last one standing there.

She was smiling, hesitant; she was in the center as she was used to be by now. It was exhilarating! Spotlight on her bright self. From all sides, her theatre chums kept calling, "Helga! Here! Helga! Come sit here! No, not there! Here! With us!"

She looked around then looked back in a brisk double-take and stayed there, mesmerized. A pair of dark eyes stopped her breath. The pupils were so big that the dark gray irises practically vanished.

People sitting next to the large black pupils followed her look. Helga smiled in an immediate, excited curiosity. Those who noticed took the situation into their own hands. "Here, Helga! Come sit here!"

There was no way to get to that vacant chair around the long, already crowded table. But this was a theatre crowd. A family in that sense. Her eyes were holding on those two dark dots. She had forgotten about everyone with whom she'd stepped into this pub.

Helga was suddenly lifted up and swayed forward across the tabletop. "Up you go!" As if her spontaneous, joyous laughter created a miraculous tunnel. She flew through, with her professional bravado, and slipped undetected by envy and malice.

A gallant arm helped her sit down. Without ever looking away from her eyes, his hand clutched hers and stayed. "Marcel. How do you do?" Her hand didn't make any effort to leave; like his eyes, his palm was already part of her.

"I'm Helga..." Noise covered the rest of her sentence. Marcel bent forward to catch her words. But it was of no importance to either of them anymore.

Time was running forward. They tried to socialize, to eat, to drink; unable to communicate with friends sitting around them; balancing on the outside of their small Universe that happened to the two of them unplanned, was all of the other life.

They left into the night. No goodbyes. Their plates stayed; supper left unfinished, knives and forks pointed towards different directions; their wine glasses half full.

Only a few, sitting in close proximity around them, had noticed. Some with mixed feelings. Some with amused faces.

Marcel and Helga couldn't care less.

Gerda's father—the banker, Carl Sommer—pushed himself up from a low red leather armchair. He put *The Financial Times* on the small side-table. It landed with a flat smack, which didn't satisfy his aim to create a poignant head-turning exclamation mark.

His hands pushed mercilessly into the pockets of his velvet house jacket. They stretched them down towards the fine Persian carpet with angry force.

His jacket didn't give way. Deep purple, it was lined with black moiré silk; bespoke, well-made. The stitches gave only a slight sigh. This sturdy frock could have easily belonged to the youth of his father. The front was buttoned in the fashion of Hungarian uniform and echoed his brief stint in the Austro-Hungarian army. It bore no resemblance to the latest fashions.

Just like the furniture in this room, Carl Sommer had ignored all of the -isms which arrived in quick sequence to the Vienna of post-war Europe.

"He did it again!" His face was a mix of shock, admiration, and annoyance. "How on Earth does he know these things?"

A little boy playing with his wooden cars on the floor looked up. "Who, Papa?"

"It's *we* . . . *We* are the bankers. It's *us* who know money! What do they know? They are just some ancient gentry . . . landowners!"

"Who, Papa?" repeated the boy, waiting for his answer.

"Marcel Van Getz," exhaled the little boy's father and poured himself a glass full of port.

"What did he do, Papa?" One of the little boy's brothers was genuinely curious. It was the money running through his blood.

"He just cashed a few more millions. He must have a billion by now."

"What is a billion?" asked the little boy. His brother, a boy of about twelve, stepped towards a large globe hung in a brightly colored wooden frame.

"It is all of the steps that you would need to make in order to walk around the Earth." He pushed carefully the age-yellowed maps on a spinning orb. It used to belong to their great-grandfather.

"But it's a ball! I would fall down!" argued the little one with good logic and a barely audible giggle.

"You are not falling now, and you are somewhere"—his brother stopped the ball in question and pointed at Austria—"here!"

"Why don't I fall?"

"It's called gravity."

"What is gravity?"

Gerda's father answered for all present. "You will have to wait until you go to school, my boy; now, be good and go play outside."

His eyes followed the baby of the family. The little boy's presence, young naïveté, and endless curiosity made it easier to forget the speed of time. Gerda was in finishing school, all of his older boys off at college. Carl Sommer lit his cigar and returned to the red leather chair in the alcove. He decided not to look at *The Financial Times* again.

ACT II

Zelda crossed the side street. It was freshly washed and swept; cobblestones looked almost blue in that early morning light. When she turned the corner, the sun glared off of a tall window on the second floor of an ancient Viennese palace. She squinted and smiled. It was a fragrant, crisp beginning of the day.

She had to admit that her life had changed to her liking recently.

It was sheer luck that she rented a room from that landlady. She was a nice, motherly woman with a young girl at her side; one of five of her children who survived the influenza. The girl was a hunchback, but lovely, bright, and cheerful as you could get. She was an usher in the Old Theatre, the greatest stage of operetta in Vienna. She told Zelda about the audition.

Zelda frowned in the sun. She was glad that she didn't go to live with her aunts in Linz. Now her plans were clear. She had her hopes set high.

Only if it weren't for her stage fright. But it'll go away! She was certain of it.

Vienna's Old Town was bustling with farmers coming from the countryside to sell their produce. You could catch the whiff of cinnamon as they were unpacking seductive bundles of apple strudels. The air was saturated with butter and sugar turned into caramel. It was oozing out from apples baked in fresh, crispy pastries.

Zelda's mouth watered. She hadn't had any breakfast. Dinner last night was a mere well-rested roll and a glass of red.

"Ouch!" A man running through the market hit Zelda's shoulder.

"Thief!" A young country girl's voice followed the running swindler. "He stole my apples!" She was pointing across the blue painted stands full of fruit baskets.

The young man turned and tossed one of the apples in Zelda's direction. "Catch!"

Her face lit up in surprise. She skillfully caught the flying fruit, gave a delighted shriek, and bit into the juicy crispy orb. There. Nobody could claim it now.

"If this isn't our Zelda." A smoothly shaved face appeared from nowhere. Zelda instinctively pressed the apple to her left hand and hid it behind her skirt. Her head tilted backwards; her eyes changed their shape from round to slits.

She was standing face-to-face with trouble. Zelda always seemed to bump into Percy in the most unusual places. His unashamed face moved close to hers "My, my, my . . ."

It was always like this; she was sick of him! Percy pulled slightly away. His eyes were judging her new appearances. "Hmm. Look at you. . ."

They used to play as children back in Chicago. She didn't like him anymore. She saw him hit a man backstage in Philadelphia. *I demand respect!* she'd heard Percy shout. She'd never thought of it, until now. Who knows if the man survived Percy's brutal attack? She wouldn't have admitted it but she'd always feared him.

A young man, about Zelda's age, stepped forward from the side of the market booth; he had stood there through the previous scene unobserved. He tossed the rest of his pretzel.

"Is there a problem, miss?" he said as loud as he was able to. Then, so that everybody around could hear him, he asked Zelda, "Do you need me to call the policeman?"

There's always a small crowd ready to assist, to call "Police!" Someone did.

Percy hissed into Zelda's face "I'll find you!" He wrenched the apple out of her hand and ran away.

Zelda saw a policeman coming and wasn't willing to stay either. "I'm so sorry," was for the young man. She pushed her way through the small gathering in the opposite direction than the heavy steps of the policeman. She didn't even look up to register the young man's amused face.

Helga was leafing through her notebook. It was stuffed with notes. Some from the girls in the finishing school. She saved those that had an unusual message. Even if it was an irritating one. Like this one. Helga flipped it open.

When this note came to Helen, as she was then, with a little box of home-made chocolates, she was genuinely surprised.

'Helen! I hear you are off to "Red Vienna." Are you mad? What do you want with those crazy radicals?' *Radicals? What is she talking about?* Helga still doesn't have the answer. Just like all other finishing schools in neutral Switzerland the politics of the World were kept at arm's length at Helga's. Politics have never been her forte anyway.

When she heard that *art is a strong politicum* over glass of red the other day, she was honestly vexed.

In the theatre crowd's favorite Winestube! She looked around hoping nobody would ask her anything. She had no opinion. 'Red Vienna'. *So what?*

She took to Vienna because of the amazing fabric designs their art teacher wore. "Vienna Werkstätte," she called them. Helen wanted to find out about those workshops; go every day, pick a scarf or a coat. Have a true Viennese coffee at the "Fledermaus" Cafe. Only after that she learned about the exciting theatre scene. But politics? Are you mad? She wished for some kind of equality, and women's rights. Although she wasn't completely clear what it meant. But to go and fight in an organized way, to march in streets and risk smelly cells at the police station? No, thank you. She liked her independence. There was freedom in money and she enjoyed every aspect of it.

Marcel seemed to have only one aim_money. It was fine with her. His next interest was her, Helga.

"I have to kiss you in the Maze!" *Oh, Marcel.* The note was written on a torn corner of a newspaper. Helga wondered if it was *The Financial Times.*

She re-read it. He really said "...in the Maze"

Her excitement was tainted by light fear. That was new! Thrilling.

She already had a drawer full of Marcel's little love notes:

"I need to kiss you in the garden."

"I have to kiss you before the second act."

"I must. . . I have to. . . I long to . . .

The Maze, the passage, the mysterious underground of the Old Theatre. Nicknamed for the chaos created by the old pieces of scenery. It held remnants of different stage designs from the vast repertory of this grand operetta house—props stored in cardboard boxes, packets of long shawls tied with hemp strings, boxes of brocade curtains, and twisted golden ropes and tassels in wooden cotton-lined trunks.

"You know there was a murder there once?"

It was only a few weeks into Helga's engagement here when she heard it for the first time; she was walking through the passage to the theatre cafe with her new friends when they blurred it out. They all laughed when she accelerated her steps. She'd stayed clear of that space since.

Helga surprised herself now. She was ready to go down there alone__to meet Marcel.

She tapped her rouge off her lips with a small strip of makeup cloth. A few drops of her perfume behind her ears, and a few more on each wrist. Finishing school was coming handy in the most unusual way.

She walked down to the atrium garden; a partly hidden side entrance took her on the staircase. There she was already halfway to the Maze. A cough came from the space ahead. Helga smiled. The stairway curved in front of her before spiraling to the underground. More noise. She felt the wave of warmth washing over this whole afternoon. "Marcel?"

A tired man's voice, his nasal consonants attesting to his hay fever, mumbled something about rat poison. "Stay away, miss. I am about to post it upstairs. It'll take a few days."

"Thank you. I was just curious . . . not walking down at all."

She turned, and her heels were tearing the stone steps as if this was all their fault.

"Miss Helga! I have something for you." Franz Hirsch, the favorite men's head-dresser, was standing at the door of her dressing room. He winked at her. She didn't like him. He fished in his vast grey overalls. He always smelled of tangerines. That she liked. Bruno says that no one can cut a men's suit like he can.

Helga recognized her beaded porte-monnaie from the old production of the Merry Widow. She gave it to Marcel when the run was over. He had a very sexual remark about the way it opened. She stopped blushing by now. "Yes?"

"Marcel said that here's a message in it." Everyone here knew Baron Van Getz well. He became 'Marcel' for the whole troupe of the Old Theatre. He spends days here during rehearsals.

Helga opened the tiny three-coin purse. It was hard not to think of Marcell's provocative innuendo.

Now the red lining was ruined by a violet ink of Marcel's pencil: *Hellas*! One word.

"Is that all? "Helga couldn't believe it.

"Yes."

"He didn't say anything else?"

Franz stared and then his thoughts clumped together "Oh, yes! He said, 'she knows where to find me'."

Come, come, come. . . Helga's chant was syncopated with her red heel impatiently hitting the floor.

Marcel's butler picked up the phone. *Finally!* It was a message she wasn't ready for" No, miss, he's not here. He was sincerely sorry. His lordship went to see his father. No further message."

Helga didn't know what to think. Her annoyance merged with jealousy. Fortunately, she came up with a quick answer; "Would you tell Marcel that I called__to cancel?"

Marcel, a gun on an angle in front of him, one eye closed, he waited then pulled the trigger. Short cracks of the gunshots finished his afternoon's diversion. The clay pigeons were shattered to pieces.

He handed the weapon to his father's servant. "All right, I've had enough."

"Excellent! You've improved, son." His father gave bubbly chuckles and kept puffing from his short pipe. "You've become a great shot since the last time we saw you." Marcel bowed his dark blond head in accord. He wasn't certain if his father's "we" meant that the old man finally slipped unreservedly into his megalomania. *We* as in "We—the Emperor." He's had the inclination.

"We'd like to see you more hunting . . . the real stuff. Deer, wild boar, bears."

"I don't have your zest for trophies, sir." That was daring. But Marcel was in a good position; he'd made a lot of money last year.

He came as soon as his father called. He didn't fuss about the fact that there was no emergency as it was presented to him over the phone. He was irritated at first. Helga must have a theory about his trip by now. Nothing he could control. He was here so better focus on his aging parent.

"A young man like you should be multifaceted. Look at your brothers . . ."

"I made myself worthwhile in the bank."

"The bank!" His father couldn't disagree more. "We are the Van Getz, not some . . . some Rothschild . . . or Sommer! All those . . . moneymakers." His pipe didn't taste good any longer. He knocked the short, round bowl on his heel until the tobacco fell out. Still burning and smoking on the ground, its smell was slowly turning into a stench. The oldest Baron Van Getz was always easily upset.

He pointed toward the chestnut alley with his hand, clutching the meerschaum. His side burns were almost white, Marcel suddenly noticed. Their position changed as the old Van Getz had no intention to conceal his satisfaction. His renewed good humor belonged to Marcel's brothers; they were leaving for a day in the forests.

"Look at them!" He watched his offspring across the manicured lawn. They were walking in the chestnut alley before turning right to the deer trail and out of his sight. Accompanied by a pair of the estate foresters with full equipment on their shoulders and provisions in their rucksacks, all men were clad in brown and moss-green hunting jackets; hats with elk teeth and feathers, short leather knickers, good thick knee-socks, and sturdy leather shoes for hiking; they looked like a hunting scene from his Black Forest mechanical toys collection.

Their dogs were impatiently running around, their rusty bodies shining through the fresh afternoon air. Autumn was slowly turning leaves and grasses into the seasonal palette of reds, ochres, and browns.

Marcel loved his game only on a plate with a good, thick fragrant sauce. That was as far as his excitement for hunting went. He would shoot rabbits in the park occasionally, but he hated the idea of feathers splashed against the sky, a little pheasant in the last pulses of his short life. The tiny body in the serving dish! It had to be stuffed with ham, pork, and spices, wrapped in a thick slice of bacon so that you could actually find it.

"Did you say your goodbyes to your brothers?"

Marcel nodded. "Yes, sir, I did."

The old baron kept looking in the distance. "Mother would have been proud."

"Thank you, father—sir."

"She always thought men should be hunters." Then he registered Marcel who'd just understood his mistake. "You are still here?"

Marcel stopped existing for Father the moment he moved to the financial world. Father would 'exercise him' from time to time. Like today. To see if his word still exudes power over his son. But never thought it necessary to offer any soothing, friendly word to him.

"You may kiss me goodbye, now. I won't see you in the morning. I read late and then____

Marcel bent and, as was customary, kissed his father's hand.

"Go, go. I will tell our Agatha to have some of my honey ready for you in the morning."

Marcel bowed and left. His long steps carried him hurriedly towards his ancestral home—a keep more than a chateau; an enclosed ring of heavy thick-walled buildings, white-washed with marks of water seeping underneath the façade into the sandstone all the way to the second floor.

No wonder his Italian mother—a young woman from Trieste—died here of rheumatic fever. The Adriatic Sea . . . His fondest memory was of the one and only holiday with his Mama . . . the white beaches . . . the azure water. Warmth.

By the time he reached the house, his plan was made. A vacation! He'll take Helga the first moment she'll be able to travel. She has her plans but will cross them all out in her calendar.

Adriatic Sea with Marcel—that was a no-brainer.

Helga's 'No, thank you' hurt him more than he wanted to admit. Marcel didn't leave without her but for the next couple of weeks became unusually busy.

Gerda was all packed. That went well! She loved to outsmart her father every chance she had. Her greatest ally, her mother, understood perfectly. Her device was brilliant.

But still, the objective of it all remained Gerda's secret. She'll trick them all in the end. She was nervous but proud of herself.

By now, her brothers were all doing their studies in different universities in Germany, in England—economics, trade, international politics.

She tried to keep up with them but had no luck. In the end, it was agreed she might spend some years in one of the best finishing schools in Switzerland.

She spoke multiple languages; could make herself a dress; learned how to knit, crochet, embroider; and could crack an egg with one hand. Back at home, she was slowly stirred toward matrimony.

Last days she had to use all of her diplomacy to get what she planned to have. Her mother's scheme in place she thought she'd be more confident. Her hands turned cold as she knocked on father's door.

"Yes, Gerda, darling?" Father was sitting at the large mahogany writing desk.

The crystal and gilt-bronze inkwell in the head of his desktop, colorful pen holders in the silver container, all in absolute order, like a devoted army waiting for the first order, then_Attack! His body leaned forward; his elbows rested on the green leather top. He folded the newspaper he was reading and set it aside.

His daughter was home from finishing school in Switzerland for good. He knew that the time was coming to choose her a husband. He wasn't ready for that. Look at her! She's just a school-girl.

"Papa, I'd like your opinion . . . may I come in?" Without waiting for her father's invitation, Gerda walked up to his desk. She leaned against the desktop, her hands on the green leather. He noticed that they were not as fine as he remembered them. Sports!

"Papa, I'm afraid. . . I need to ask you a favor . . ."

"Allowance . . . ?"

Gerda blushed. "No—Oh, Papa!"

He pointed at the green leather upholstered chair. She loved that piece.

She decided not to sit down. "I've been wondering, if"—then she said briskly—"if I could enroll in a university, just for the new semes—"

"University! What for? Absolutely not!" He got up from his chair and started walking in front of the heavily dressed window. "You are rich. I give you everything you need to be happy . . . don't I?" He paused. Gerda wasn't saying anything, but he knew her pauses well. *Like her mother.* Her face turned crimson, her chin protruding forward. *Like her grandmother.*

He didn't want to give in. He knew his answer to all that women's intellectual nonsense. He was engaged once before he married Gerda's mother. His fiancée went, "Just for a semester." She'd never come back! He had it with intellectuals. She was a scientist by now. He heard that she received her *venia legendi,* the teaching license. She has been teaching men! Disaster!

It still made him angry. Women. They are for men's pleasure—to bear children, to represent their husband. "University? No. Ask me anything but that."

"But father—"

"I said no."

Gerda curtsied and walked out. He watched her stepping on the terrace then walking down to the lake. *She'll calm down. They all always do.*

He suddenly noticed how tall she'd grown, how athletic. Those tennis, rowing, shooting, swimming, riding lessons—that all had shaped that young woman into . . . into . . . a thin, muscular, practically flat-chested athlete. That was definitely not the shape which had attracted him to her mother! Modern times. The Great War had changed everything.

But! It had brought a lot of money to his bank. War is a business. He couldn't complain. Even the largest financial swing in the world was unable to diminish his wealth. There were only a handful like him. *Why did we stop inviting that genius Van Getz to our home?* He will ask his wife tonight. Sheer money-wizard, that young man. He wondered *Could we lure him. . . ?* Gerda's mother said, *Absolutely not.* He was shocked over the story she told him.

It still lingered the next day when he took his eleven o'clock gnash; he couldn't wrap his head around it. *Van . . . Getz . . . to our Gerda?*

A promise was a promise; he never mentioned that unpleasant business to his wife again.

Gloria herself knew well what she thought about Vienna_Opera! Her dream.

Now she could make it happen for her daughter. She had to laugh at how that young, bright girl thinks that her mother doesn't know about her theatre ambitions. Her own blood! There is a talent in her veins. Just like when Gloria was a young woman.

Times were different then; she wasn't allowed to go anywhere— not by her conservative, catholic, family. Yet she did! Successfully. Behind their back she got an audition and_ got a serious offer from the opera directors! It's all in the good device.

Gloria sang beautifully. Her voice was exceptional, her parents' guests would always compliment her. She always danced well. It was so natural for her. Oh, those balls! All night 'til dawn, to the right, sway forward, backward, and to the left—the waltz! It was smooth, breathtaking, beyond exciting. *Like making love to Marcel.* She glanced in fear at her husband. Rain created transparent lace curtains of raindrops on the conservatory glass walls. Carl was napping.

She was safe. She wasn't sure that her words stayed only within her thoughts. *Where there's Marcel, there's no safety for me.* She wanted to get rid of everything which could remind her of him. Yet. She didn't. She'll do it tonight.

Gloria put down her knitting. "Darling . . . Gerda tells me that—"

Carl Sommer was wide awake in an instant "No. I'm sorry. I've told you."

He quickly carried the full tea cup to his mouth. Tea was cold! His voice graduated to a higher tone. Louder too. "You know my opinion." The cup and saucer sounded his frustration on the small round ebony table. Tea splashed the polished top. "It's final. You both know it." He tossed the white napkin on top of the spill. It started making brown maps on the fine linen.

"Oh, we do!" His wife, Gloria, decided not to notice. Her cause was too important. She picked up her knitting and moved across from him in a loveseat. "This is about her desire to take serious singing lessons in Vienna, darling. She'd like to travel a little bit before we find her a suitable husband."

That was a different story. Carl Sommer sat up straight "I knew she'd come to her senses. She's my smart girl!"

"Yes, my dear . . . and she loves you very much!" Gloria's needles kept busy.

"I presume you selected the teacher wisely. What does it cost me?"

Gloria had no idea but chose intelligently her husband's way of doing things," She'll try first, pay last!"

Carl Sommer heard his favorite saying and was flattered. "Who would have thought? Vienna. Her voice certainly deserves attention." He returned to his cold tea. "Would you ring for Jan, dear?"

"May I tell her she has your blessing, or would you prefer to give her the news yourself?"

"I'll do it, it's not a problem."

His wife rang the bell. Their reliable valet came in and saw her smile. Success then.

"Would you tell Miss Gerda to come here, please?"

"Bring us some Tokaji, Jan. It's three o'clock, after all. And take the tea away."

"You always know best, my darling!" Gloria's adoring bright smile caressed her husband; she blew him a kiss.

"Time to celebrate!" Carl Sommer slapped his palms together. His signet ring reflected the one and only sunray that made it through the curtains of rain that afternoon.

"Fly!" was the message Gloria embroidered white on white on a handkerchief for Marcel. It was over between them before she gave it to him. Her cipher "G" was in the corner to remind him of her. Her perfectly manicured fingers with many rings carried it to the étagère now.

In a round heavy clear crystal flacon was her favorite French perfume. She pulled out the long, icicle resembling stop and let one drop seep in the tip of the fine fabric.

Carl Sommer was coming down with a cold. He couldn't believe it! His bi-annual indisposition on the day of his daughter's departure! He sent her white orchids with a little gift_ a golden chain with a miniature of Saint Gertrude and a brief note _VeniVidiVici.

Gerda immediately sent him a Thank you note: I am going to see and I'll win for you, Papa.

Next morning, when kissing her daughter at the station, Gloria placed the embroidered handkerchief in Gerda's hand. "Here, darling, I made it for. . ." she hesitated before her ambivalent "Good Luck" helped her cover the lie.

Gerda lifted the small square in the air and inhaled the whiff; "Your favorite scent, Mama! Jasmine. How sweet of you. You'll be around me in Vienna."

Gloria suddenly regretted her decision. What has been a memento became a double parting present. An inexplicable need to hear his name was overwhelming. *Just this last time!*

She smiled and said matter-of-factly:

"Do you remember Marcel?"

Gerda's knuckles crushed the handle of her hatbox. "Who?" Her foot stepped back on the platform.

"Never mind." Mother struggled to reattach her veil.

Gerda watched her mother's face with utmost alarm.

"Is he someone important?"

"No." said Mother with _ was it a hint of sorrow? Something seemed to be bothering her in the shoe. She was bent forward fixing the problem when she said,

"He was. . . a friend. Long gone." Her face was red once she reemerged. But it seemed natural after she was head down. Gloria hoped the old trick worked.

"Aha. I don't think I remember. Is he dead?"

That's all Gloria needed to hear. She realized these last few hours that the one thing she wasn't ready for was Marcel's presence in her daughter's life.

"Yes, he is." She lifted her veil and gave her daughter a warm kiss,

"Bon Voyage, Gerda, my darling. Bonne chance!"

ACT III

————— ◦◦◦✦◦◦◦ —————

Outdoor market was in its afternoon peak. Zelda was looking for some good sweet plums. The noisy crowd reminded her of her last unpleasant meeting with Percy—the last time Zelda saw Percival Best prior to that, he was Percy the Best for his vaudeville act.

She was surprised that the boy, who used to climb into her garden to steal the first cherries, was now here in Vienna. He would periodically frustrate all of the starlings of Chicago.

People of the art world flocked like birds and left for places which the previous generations ran away from. Zelda was back in her fatherland.

It has been known about Percy that he had always been involved in some kind of shady business. Once, she overheard that he'd had his fingers in drug dealing. It came to Zelda with absolute clarity now. Cocaine, they said.

Zelda found some plums, almost translucent in the autumn light. She bought some purple ones with 'dust'. Those were ripe for sure. Their juicy amber insides were the highlight of the plum season.

She couldn't help but smile. Her income was steady now. Although, it was still a question: fruit or sweets? Zelda shined one of the gorgeous chubby plums on the side of her overcoat. She closed her eyes and__The sweet shower sprinkled her cheeks. She fished for her checkered handkerchief. Just in time! The juices started running down her chin; the concert of tastes was__

"I knew I'd found you here!" Zelda was face-to-face with Percy.

This was not up to him to interrupt her precious moment. She turned away.

"I'm talking to you!" Percy's hand hit hers, and the delicious plum took to the air, smashing to mush a few feet away.

Zelda didn't hesitate this time. "Help!" was a scream well-formed in her diaphragm, strong and loud at the top of her lungs. Percy stepped back. The crowd of market shoppers moved forward.

Zelda pointed at Percy with the theatricality of one playing a new scene; as if a full, bright spotlight was on her, she said, "Him!"

She gave a small dramatic pause, "He hit me!" was even louder. She looked around.

You would have expected Percy to turn towards the audience and start singing.

But he did not.

A policeman appeared from nowhere. He stood there, pounding his left palm meaningfully with the baton attached to his right wrist. "Any problem here?"

Percy was already running away. Before he zoomed around the jovial cop, he made a shout to Zelda. "I'll find you again! Don't worry."

She started crying. "Did he steal money from you?" The policeman took out a small, bent notebook in a tired black leather cover. He licked the top of his short ink pencil. It left a deep purple mark on his tongue.

"I . . . I don't know." Zelda quickly decided to lie. Her act continued. She opened her arms as if she suddenly noticed what had happened: "I . . . I think . . . yes . . . My purse is missing."

The policeman looked her deeply in her eyes; "You want to make a statement, Fräulein?"

Zelda felt his look, experienced by years on the street, piercing right through her. Did he recognize her from the last time? She blew her nose, then shook her head 'no.'

"No, eh?" He had swayed back and forth on the heels of his boots. They gave several creaks. He was not amused. "You've been wasting my time, girl!"

"Go home!" He turned to the curious onlookers. "There's nothing for you here. Shoo! Away, away!"

The crowd, robbed of their daily dose of amusing distraction, started merging back into the joyful chaos of the open market.

"Would you care for something sweet?" A young man, about Zelda's age, stepped forward from the side of the market booth. He tossed the rest of the apricot he was chewing on. "For the birds."

She realized that it was the same place where she saw him the last time. "Have you been standing there since we. . .?"

He, too, recognized her, although she was dressed in new fashions.

"Yes." He squinted, smiling broadly "Evidently. Waiting for you. How else?"

They laughed. Zelda calmed down.

A pleasant, cleanly shaved face, brown hair peeking from under his hat—he was dressed simply in a brown two-part suit. He took off his brown homburg for her. Zelda liked that. She hoped someone was watching.

"How about that café over there?" The young man pointed across the canal. "May I invite you for a slice of their *Sachertorte?*"

Zelda couldn't resist. Today was her "fruit day." There were no coins left for the sweets in her small beige porte monnaie this week. She dared to suggest, "Perhaps a nice slice of *Linzertorte?*"

"Sure. They make a great Linzer; the lattice work is never burnt." His amused smile was a good sign. "They give a generous cloud of whipped cream too. It's the best in town!"

Zelda relaxed. The young stranger stretched his arm forward. "Jacob Holzknecht, at your service."

The theatre house was dark and devoid of the audience, the stage sparsely lit. It was the orchestra pit which had a strong spotlight on, and was busy.

"Let's try it again with the new cast. I will ask Misters Grösch and Holzknecht to take their places." The conductor nodded to the newcomers: "You did very nicely in our rehearsal yesterday; come, find those lovely notes for me now."

The company watched, amused. They all knew the process. Maestro Kremer, the conductor in the Old Theatre in Vienna, was a friendly man; most of them had their debut under his baton.

Some still remembered the late Hubert. Perhaps more musical than Kremer, a sweet man too. Tragic end. But who would recall such a horror. They tucked it to the back of their memory. The newcomers never heard of him.

Zelda was late for the rehearsal as usual, and lucky, too. Her group hadn't been called yet. She took off her overcoat and dropped it over the closed basket she'd brought with her today. In it were carefully folded shirts she irons for the head-dresser Franz Hirsch to earn some extra money.

The song was over, Maestro Kremer invited his new tenors to confer with him from the edge of the stage. He turned towards them, half of his torso above the orchestra pit, he faced them calmly giving corrections in his usual tactful manner. Once finished, his face turned up and his loud "Very well then!" sent towards the gilded ceiling was a sign to everyone else that he was ready to continue.

A pleasant, high, surprised female voice shouted across the stage "Jacob!" Everybody looked up. But Jacob didn't mind, and neither did Zelda, the soprano.

"Stay calm, dear child, or we'll have to call firemen." The well-rounded baritone of Maestro Kremer's voice made everybody laugh.

Only Zelda detected a slight hint of impatience. "Sorry," she peeped, and merged with the other girls. She still had a second to smile at her new acquaintance. He stepped offstage and was now standing in the first wing. Zelda forgot to be nervous.

The orchestra of the Viennese Old Theatre put their instruments at the ready. Nothing could please Maestro Kremer more than Strauss. Bruno Gottlieb listened from his office. He missed his friend Hubert. It cost Bruno some extra theatre tickets to keep that murder under wraps. Life. The orchestra sounded better than ever. *The show must...* he knew well.

Zelda looked at Jacob. She hasn't noticed before that he was actually . . . quite dashing . . .

"This soliloquy is really impossible to remember!" Helga dropped her arm by her side, the thin paperback clutched between her fingers; she closed her eyes. "Ah." Her head dropped back on the thick collar of one of Marcel's lush Turkish-cotton bathrobes. Wrapped in the white luxury, she began stumbling over her lines one more time.

"Put it down, sleep on it."

"I have to learn it, or I'll forget how to use my brain."

"Come to bed…There's something I want to memorize . . . acutely." Marcel's voice got into dangerous velvety low tones. Not just because his suntan made him look different, Helga lost the remnant of strong will to resist him. She laughed and dropped the poor Molière on the white sofa.

Marcel held the silky blanket open until her naked body slipped under and pressed against his. She felt his abundant curls attacking the lower of her back. Her soliloquy came to her now, uninvited: the words, their rhythm. She began humming the lines, working her way forward through the full long speech, her body surrendered to the rhythm of iambic pentameter without ever being suspected. When she finally lost the words, she sincerely believed Molière would have liked the circumstance.

Early morning began behind the white curtains, decorated with black silk tassels, without rush. The quiet garden was pierced with the first morning bird song.

"My rehearsal! "Helga sat up straight from her deep sleep. Shock catapulted her from the warm bed. She started running.

Marcel reached for his white telephone. "Prepare my car . . . ten minutes." He slowly set up and dropped his legs to the carpet.

"Ten minutes? I can't be ready in ten minutes." Helga's voice, now muffled by the shower door exuded honest panic. She turned off the water and as wet as she was ran to the dressing room.

Marcel's Lagonda was like a lightning bolt. Helga, wet hair, no makeup, was trying to put on rouge. *In the speeding car? Silly idea!* Sudden changes of the road surface made her attempts unattainable. She pulled down the travelling spectacles over her eyes and moved lower in the black leather seat.

She should call her drama teacher, Camille. They said to each other "we'll keep in touch" when she was leaving Switzerland. Helga truly meant it. She was always sincere about her friendships; but not very good at following through. Camille Ami was the reason why she fell in love with drama. She was as lovely as her name.

Camille taught them how to use their voices without ruining them, how to breathe. It wasn't part of the curriculum, but she was once an aspiring actress; her dream was shattered together with her ankle. On the other hand, her slight limp gave her enough respectability that she was hired by the school board. Lucky for Helga. No, she can't contact her yet. Operetta was nothing her teacher respected. For Helga this was the perfect lucky start. She looked at her lover through the small mirror of her silver powder compact. He gave her this delicately chiseled square, the exact size of her palm. She'd have never met Marcel if it were not for the Old Theatre operetta. He was not one for drama; she knew it now; on stage or off. "We should try again. What do you think?" It took Helga a moment to register his question "Try what?"

Marcel, his eyes carefully on the meandering road, bent his body sideways to reach Helga's ear, and whispered, "I need to have you . . ." and further teased, ". . . in the Maze."

The cafe was the Viennese symphony in black, brass and white marble: Small, round, white marble tabletops on black cast-iron bases, dark wood Thonet chairs_ like snakes made solid by some wizard; newspaper stretched in large rattan frames hung on brass wall hangers, tall black counters topped with long slabs of polished white marble, large, brass framed mirrors and tall windows inviting the outside in. It was the best of its kind in Vienna.

Jacob looked over the cup of hot chocolate at Zelda.

"I swear, I recognize your face."

She gave an audible giggle. An old woman at the next table stared her down.

"Shhh." Jacob chuckled "For real. In a newspaper."

"A newspaper? I don't think so."

Zelda was shy of being photographed. Superstitious in fact. She took another sip, savoured it for a moment, then said, without much excitement,

"That could be my father, perhaps. I do look like him." She took time to enjoy the thick dark drink. "But I doubt it. He lives in America. He's an architect. Ludo Zinger."

"That's it! "Jacob put his half full cup down on the saucer." The new theatre in Chicago. Right?"

Zelda Zinger's hand holding a chunk of tart, already her second, had dangerously tilted. "Yes." She gasped in disbelief and put the sweet helping back on the small plate. "You've heard of my father . . . that's unbelievable . . ."

Jacob waved down a waitress. "Two more hot chocolates," then looking at Zelda, he asked, "Is that all right?"

"Oh yes, yes. Thanks."

"Maybe you'd like some coffee instead?"

"No, thanks. Hot chocolate is great."

"It must have been an amazing experience to live in such a household. Tell me."

"I don't know."

"How do you mean?"

"They . . . divorced."

"Oh."

"She left him . . . She wanted a life, career. . . He had one, and thought it was good for both."

The envelope in Zelda's pocket was green; it was covered with pictures of animals running around and peeking out from behind the corners. Zelda drew them with colored pencils. It was a reminder of her mother.

"She didn't want to be bothered. By. . . by mundane life."

"Your father is such a talented man, if you don't mind me saying that now."

"No, I don't mind."

It was a letter Zelda wrote to her mother, as a ten-year-old girl, from a sanatorium in the mountains. It came back, without any answer, all of Zelda's grammatical errors corrected, in a red pen. In the place of greetings was a red exclamation mark.

Zelda's eyes went blank for a moment. Jacob wasn't sure what just happened. His sensitivity observed that his curiosity took this young woman to places where he had no business to tread. Zelda's eyes found Jacob. "He writes to me, sometimes . . . Nice letters. He's been all right. How's your chocolate?"

"It's fine. Very." Jacob was glad to be out of that surprisingly odd conversation. His fault. He'll be more careful, next time. *What next time? Stop rushing, Holzknecht. But honestly?* He liked her more than he wanted to show. He needed to slow down; this might be merely his fantasy. Perhaps, this is it. They'll finish, pay and he will become just one of many of her theatre chums. "Anything else I could do for you?"

She sipped slowly from her white cup with painted forget-me-nots running under the glaze in a single row. Her pause was unbearable. Jacob was trying not to hang on her every movement. When she answered, it was very simple—like a little girl who asked humbly for a lollipop. "Yes. Please. Could you call me Zelli?"

Helga went through without much more than one brief knock on the open door. With a few steps in her stage pumps she walked into the office. She wished her heels could make more radical noise.

"Bruno, really? A Review? You? The King of operetta?" Her head was tossing her short bob forward with every word. She walked up to the armchair, placed in front of his desk, and dropped in it. That's where she always resided after rehearsals. Now wasn't her time. It gave a squeak in the old wooden joints. Helga, the subretta, crossed her legs. She didn't put her feet carefully on the desktop as usual. Bruno Gottlieb, the theatre director, saw the message.

He wished her on his side. He stood up from his desk and walked to her. "Everybody does it, now. C'mon, Helga! What's gotten into you?" Bruno, her friend, pulled a small armchair from the coffee table closer to her, "Come. Talk to me."

"Is that the new girl you hired? What's her name?" There was a hint of jealousy in that, wasn't there? He said as straight as he mustered, no stress on the girl's name "Adrianne."

"Adrianne." Helga nodded as she was pronouncing her name. "Is she really that good . . . or is she"—Helga's voice spiraled down to a seductive alto timber—"that good?"

She looked at him, her chin down, her large eyes larger. Bruno knew that look well.

"Ha! No! No. She's not my type."

"You don't have a type."

"You . . . bucket of poison." he winked at her. It worked.

Helga laughed. "Poison? *Moi*?"

More giggles and Bruno knew he could continue on the safe ground "You know, she's what I was waiting for: she's tall, has that angular, modern look."

"Very modern. Is she dating a sculptor?"

"Precisely, modern!" and, after a brief run through the imaginary rolodex of his brain he got lost "A sculptor? No, I don't know about that."

"She should. She can certainly personify one of the -isms."

He sat down on top of his desk "Be nice. Even the most bizarre costumes will look sensational on her!"

"Haha. A costume hanger!"

Was she starting again? Bruno bent and pulled a bottle of red from under his desk."

With a broad smile his 'Yes?' Was an invitation for a glass of wine.

"I see, you have it all planned to detail, already."

"Oh, come on, Helga. You'll love the show." Bruno handed her a short glass that used to hold mustard and put another one from that set on the table. He poured and then moved closer. He took her under his arm.

She smelled the familiar cloud of his favorite patchouli. His fatherly squeeze makes it always better; magic! Even today, again. Helga kissed his cheek. "Just don't make her cross my path . . . onstage, I mean." She put the empty glass in his hand.

"Of course, you do, dear!" laughed the director; still, Helga's friend.

As Helga was about to walk out, an impatient chorus girl, without waiting for an invitation, pushed in "Why the new stick? Why her? Why not me? Again?"

"Oh, good afternoon, Miss Waldek. And how are you?"

He turned his eyes to the low ceiling. Helga laughed in the doorway and performed a chain of dance steps chanting "Stick-a-stick-a stick-a-stick..." until she turned the corner.

It was now midafternoon; Helga was slowly walking downstairs. The slanted windows high above allowed enough light. The Maze in front of her was dimmed. She couldn't imagine walking here after dark. She tiptoed step by step making very little noise. Now she was glad the stage heels were not clicking. She wanted the moment of surprise to be perfect.

Slight noise. She failed to be first here! Oh, well. Helga paused, and listened. She heard someone's breathing among the pieces of propped scenery. She made a few steps forward, then stopped. With an amused tone she said "Marcel?" There was no answer. "Marce-el?" Light tone, almost a melody. The sound of breathing.

"Marcel, I'm waiting." Fear came like a flash flood, grasped her and held Helga's brain hostage. Regardless, she tried to talk.

"I will walk away if you don't come out." Her words were not holding together anymore. Fear was turning her hands to sweating icicles. She reached for sure help: her anger and irony.

"Now, really . . . how very exciting!"

"What is?" asked Marcel from the stairwell above her.

Helga turned, grabbed Marcel's hand, and rushed them out of there.

Jacob stood up and looked around. He needed a breather. Another of Gaston Leroux murder mysteries. His favorite series.

The amateur detective, Joseph Rouletabille, the hero, just got locked in a room without windows. "Oh, the French!"

"It's fiction, Jacob. Literature." Rubin, his old friend, teased him. "He'll get out. I read it."

"It's a series, of course he gets out! They need to make money."

"Yeah, Jacob. You should be a detective!" someone from the sun tanning theatre crowd suggested.

There was an irony in it. But he didn't care. He actually liked the thought of it.

Jacob stretched and didn't say much. But there was an idea that he'd like to spend more time investigating. There was the word! A private investigator.

The woods around their shared little cottage were young; the short trees allowed for a lot of light. Planted in exact lines they resembled chorus girls ready for their first number.

"How did your rehearsal go?" he asked in the general direction of his friends.

"It's going great." One of the girls looked up from a film magazine she just opened, "I love the costumes. I don't think I've ever worn this much glitter! Like these film stars..."

Jacob remembered Zelda's piggy-bank. She has been saving for a new costume, she said.

"I always thought they would give you all of your costumes."

Zelda looked up from her book. "That would be amazing, but no. Can we stop talking about theatre? This is our day off."

"Jacob, didn't you have to bring your own? A travel trunk, a big basket, full of your own costumes?" asked Clio, one of the chorus girls, through the small kitchen window. It had white and green painted frames and green shutters with cut hearts in their middle.

"No, they gave me my costumes." Jacob reminisced," At least for my first show." He chortled. "My last show."

They all started laughing, including Jacob. "I am not an actor, people! I admit! I wanted to try. Everybody was always telling me I had a great voice—"

"And you do!" Zelda left her book on the chair and sat on Jacob's thigh. Her voice changed to a miniscule voice of a cartoon character, "You have the voice, and you have the looks. You just. . ."

". . . Cannot act!" He finished through fits of giggles coming from all around.

She held him around his neck, and bent dangerously backwards, "But I love you even more!"

Jacob kissed her chin.

"Watermelon, people!" Clio stepped out from the cottage. She placed the tray, an old prop from some long gone operetta on the deck. Both in need of some fresh paint. The dish was full of chopped succulent delicacy. Suntanned hands were quick. Zelda laughed and picked a sumptuous slice before someone else was quicker. She bit into the red juicy flesh. No Percy here to steal it from her.

Jacob spat the small black pits in a bravura spray shot. His curious"How about the new review?" made someone say "Maybe detective is not the right thing for you. An investigative journalist, perhaps."

"Let him be! "Rubin moved in defence and answered," That's going to be different."

"Mine will be only my underwear." Zelli blushed. She quickly picked another slice of watermelon. She was about to take a bite when Jacob's mind arrived at a tangled place.

"I thought you were having some costumes made, no?" Jacob turned to her. There was all the money Zelda said she had to be putting aside.

"No, not really . . . oh! Yes. Yes, I did."

Jacob knew that she was lying. "Then what were you . . .?"

"It's a secret!" Somebody chimed among smacking noises. Then a chorus of exaggerated *Ahas* and *Hmms* and *It's a mystery!* had followed from different directions. It was humor that fell flat although Jacob played along. *A secret? But why?* He liked mysteries only on the page.

"Is there more watermelon?" Rubin tossed the dark green peel to the forest and turned his head to Clio.

"Did you bring one?" She played her smash without the slightest hesitation.

Her crowds cheered!

Zelda regained composure between two last juicy morsels. She returned to her book.

Jacob took his. *A secret.* He couldn't make himself read. Then the Jacob whom Zelli loved turned back to the facts. She might be saving for a present for him, and he behaves like an idiot.

Jacob wiped his mouth and closed his book. "Come, Zelli. Put your shoes on." He stood up." Let's go for a walk." Zelda nodded. He bent down and looked into the dark of her sunglasses.

"I think we should go out tonight when we come back to town. What do you think?" His generosity would arrive in the most perfect moments. In her mind's eye she saw her money dropping into the secret little treasure box. "Perfect!" she said lovingly out loud.

A chorus girl, sweaty from a dance number, breathing rapidly, just ran off the stage after the scene. She saw Helga getting ready for her solo and let the other girls run ahead. She came up to Helga and started talking immediately, "I am so sorry . . . for you and Marcel." She was trying to catch her breath. "Truly . . . sorry."

Helga stopped moving; she has been waiting for something like this. A girl, any girl, who would catch Marcel's heart in some inexplicable state of mind, and he would propose.

News like this, she heard, is always announced at the "best" moment. This one was hers, now. The all-male chorus was ending, then comes her intro, and then her grand solo. Let's hear it then. She turned towards the girl"Oh yeah? How do you mean?"

"I mean . . . we really didn't think."

Did the girl just say_*we*? That was worse than Helga thought.

Stage manager rushed to grab Helga. "Your intro!" She jerked her arm free. "Wait!"

The girl's voice was one tone machine-gun: "We didn't know that someone would go down there at that hour. We were making out in the Maze, me and Lorenz and you showed up."

The experienced conductor made the confused orchestra play Helga's intro one more time and_ there she was! On top of a steep flight of wide staircase, center stage, with all of her luminosity; her smile took the audience's breath away. She was standing in the full lights with a spotlight of yellows and pinks, ready for her song. Helga knew that all the jolly filters of this make-believe sunny day couldn't be brighter than her new zeal for life with Marcel.

This wasn't the blue envelope which all of the chorus girls always feared: the your-weight doesn't-comply. . . etc. etc. An ultimatum so easily issued at times like these, among the financial crisis stricken world. Hundreds of unemployed dancers would kill for an engagement at Bruno Gottlieb's theatre.

This envelope was a brown one. To Zelda this seemed to be a lose-lose situation.

The typewriter cut through it at places where the secretary's quick hand hit the key hard.

Zelda tried not to read too much into it. Yet, she still held it in her hand inside her purse. Slow to fight her fear, her heart turned into an inaudible string of life-threatening trembles.

Zelda didn't want anybody to see her tears if it was what she feared. She decided for the Imperial Greenhouse. Since it was now public, after the monarchy was abolished after the Great War, it has become a favorite of hers. No matter what the skies looked like outdoors here it was filtered through intensely green leafage of all hues of greens, blues and yellows. It made her feel better right away. Zelda chose the first empty garden chair.

She sat down on the green painted wooden seat. The black cast iron frame was cold. She moved her legs away. She hated when she couldn't control her nerves. Bruno surely noticed. Here is his letter. He must have seen it. It took all of Zelda's discipline to overcome her stage fright. It has been exhausting! Oh, grandma Zinger. If only she was still around . She was in vaudeville. Zelda remembered her stories. She would have understood. No one to share her anxieties with. No one to give Zelli the shoulder to cry on or to say 'well done!". Once up there, on the stage, she loved to perform; she loved it like nothing in her life.

But she still wasn't able to truly enjoy herself, to have fun. This is it. Bruno finally made his decision, and kicked her out. Yes. That's it. Loud and clear. Zelda took one deep breath.

Now or never. She pulled out a metal hairpin from her low chignon and tore the envelope along the short side. One quick pull, a flick of the paper and__Her eyes as bright as if one of the stage lights was shining straight at her face, Zelda's melodious, trained voice said up to the vast green space, "An understudy to Miss Helga Hayden!"

ACT IV

The new show was the talk of Vienna long before the opening night. All of the previews were sold out. Bruno Gottlieb outdid himself again. He combined everything he knew and had, and on top of it hired great talent for all the other theatrical skills which he didn't himself possess.

The result was an imaginative, entertaining show made-to-measure for Vienna. The success was tremendous.

Gerda raised a glass full of champagne to her image in the mirror. Her secret invention of the new self__ Adrianne, never failed to amuse her. Singing lessons during weekdays, and now, the successful theatre review in the evenings! Her mother's white handkerchief must have magic!

She shook her dyed-blond mane. She still couldn't believe her luck. Her very first show! In such a short time. Such fun. Her Mother's message "Fly!" made her soar to the heights she didn't dare to dream. What was the best?__She has talent!

Although, talent or not, the previews didn't go exactly smoothly at first.

When they had the first one, Gerda thought a small mishap happened. She didn't think much of it since everybody was nervous, not perfectly settled in the choreographies. But then the next day the very same thing happened again_ In the act called "Treasures of Asia," all the chorus girls wore small pagoda headpieces, made out of glittering glass beads, and held a silver wand with shimmering tassels in their hand. As they rushed around Adrianne the last girl reached out and poked her face. It was clearly not an accident.

43

Bruno Gottlieb noticed it as a mishap, since he didn't know that it had already happened before. He called the girl to the side to point out she had to be more careful.

When he saw Adrianne, after the performance, a Band-Aid close to her eye he assured her. "I saw the mishap. It won't happen again."

"Just a small accident . Nothing to worry about."

He looked at her, eyebrows up to his hairline. "Really?" He didn't buy it.

"Really . . . it's nothing," she chimed, in a good mood.

Bruno shrugged his shoulders. *One thing less to think about. Fine with me.*

The last performance of the previews arrived. Adrianne was as excited as everybody; audiences were delighted, some had already seen the show at least once. The house was packed.

One quick costume-change after another, and then there was the spectacular "Treasures of Asia" again. Adrianne stood there, bright smile, exquisite tall figure in a resplendent costume all colors of the rainbow. The moment came and the 'tail' of the Chinese dragon was passing by her; the line of girls with glittering pagodas of beads crowning their heads started their last run moving close, around Adrianne, before exiting the stage. Adrianne saw it first! The silver wand was ready in the girl's hand to charge against her eyes.

The second before Bruno could scream, before the chorus girl delivered her poke, Adrianne shot her arm and firmly grasped the wand. She didn't stop laughing, her smile shining, she was obviously in a glorious mood. She caught the girl's arm. Without showing the slightest effort, she jerked the girl sideways with such force that she disconnected her from the running line of girls.

They didn't notice, they had vanished into the wings, running as fast as they could for their next costume change.

The conductor spotted what just happened. On his command: "Encore!"

The orchestra caught up with their notes and played the vivacious music of the last scene all over again.

Adrienne pulled the wand abruptly from the shocked girl's hand. To the new round of the bright, cheerful music Adrienne started waving the magic wand from left to right and back again. With swift theatrical gestures, in the tempo of quick four, laughing out loud, she obliterated girl's headpiece to hundreds of little, glittering beads and shreds while cascades of laughter from the audience created the most agreeable backdrop all the way to the final forte of the orchestra! Deafening laughter still going after the bare headed, disheveled chorus girl ran screaming off stage, Adrianne repositioned herself on her pedestal, and to the enormous thunderous applause the curtain came down.

"She has guts, that girl!" Bruno turned to his stage manager. He slapped his thighs and roared with laughter.

"Who has guts?" Asked Marcel, who just arrived backstage. He saw the first preview. It was enough for him; tonight he "couldn't come sooner."

"You've missed the greatest fun!"

Marcel spotted Helga getting ready for her solo; her petticoat, with white and red ruffles, over her head as she bent forward to adjust laces on her red boots. "I don't think I have!" He said, coyly, and winked at Bruno. He didn't wait for any answer and rushed through the side door to his box.

Champagne was ordered already well ahead; Marcel planned a sensational party in his small château outside Vienna.

Everybody there was feeling like a star. The new girl was at center stage even here. Her name was Adrianne, Marcel learned. She was thin, sporty, more muscular than voluptuous. Nothing that would have ever interested him before. And a chorus girl at that. Only that the first stains of the midlife crisis started coloring his nights.

His relationship with Helga was ticking steadily. It was a safe haven to retreat to. She's as good a player as he is. Nothing to fear. He could be sure of her habits: Helga wasn't coming in for at least the first hour, he knew that for a fact.

She would celebrate in the theatre right after the show, go home, shower, put on fresh make-up, change into something divine, and make her entrance when the party was at its best.

This was the new girl's first opening night. She was overwhelmed by her success. Although still learning the trade, they say that she had just arrived from some unpronounceable town in Hungary, she was the it girl tonight. Marcel was enchanted. She was an athlete, a good dancer; her voice was a pleasant. . . was it a *mezzo?* guessed Marcel.

Her hair was combed into a sleek, blond bob; he could easily picture her with two braids, dressed in a folk dress, working her way up in a vineyard. He tossed his cigarette.

"Hi, what's your name?"

Gerda couldn't believe that Marcel didn't recognize her. At first, she thought that he was pretending; but no. She's grown up out of the image of the little girl with cherries around her ears. She decided to enjoy this incognito as long as she could: "Adrienne. What's yours?" This was too much fun to reveal herself to him now.

"Marcel."

"Marcel who?"

"Is that important?"

"I guess not."

"You are not wasting any time, deary," slurred one of two passing chorus girls in her direction. Both dressed in their glittering best, already sufficiently intoxicated. Champagne was never in short supply at Marcel's. Gerda ignored them and didn't lose her focus.

"Have you been enjoying yourself onstage?" asked Marcel quickly.

"I was so nervous; I almost fainted." That was the truth.

"I know that feeling! I tried once, but it's not for me." He laughed.

"What's for you?" She was truly curious how much he changed.

"Numbers, figures . . . speculations, money . . . Will you wait here? Have some champagne. I'll be right back!"

No, he hasn't changed. She was secretly beaming. Father would like him.

Somebody placed a new record on the gramophone; the whole room burst out in Charleston.

Marcel came back and the music changed into a slow foxtrot. "May I, Adrianne?" He opened his arms. *You may. Anything,* Gerda thought. As he spun her around slowly, Marcel noticed her perfume. French, no doubt. It smelled two social classes above a chorus girl . . . unless . . . unless she has a wealthy lover. There was a challenge. Marcel was interested.

They danced one time around then Marcel took them to the sideline and stopped; she didn't have the time to feel hurt. He bent to kiss her hand and whispered, "I'll wait for you." She felt a rough push in her palm—a small piece of paper.

She wasn't sure how he meant it. He turned, his look seemed to share a secret with her. Before she was able to think it through he walked out.

Gerda went to powder her nose. In a spacious lilac and silver room she opened her palm. The note said, "I need to kiss you, now, in the maze."

She walked back in the ballroom and looked around. People in small groups were all celebrating. She walked up to a waiter. "Excuse me, I heard there is a maze in this house . . ."

"No, not in the house, miss. It's down in the garden."

"Oh, then I guess I won't be able to see it tonight," and she took another glass of champagne from the small, mirror-lined silver tray.

When she was certain that nobody was looking, Gerda slowly walked out on the large terrace. Everybody was inside or in front where buffet tables were extended to pamper everyone.

One more inconspicuous glance around. She was safe to descend the broad concrete staircase without any witness. She walked across the uneven lawn in her fine heels until she reached the dark wall of yews. The park was much larger than one could suspect from the house.

Her excitement was building up; she forgot to be worried. She was standing in front of the maze, the dark structure was tall, overwhelming. Her excitement, tangible. She was prepared to take what she knew had always belonged to her. Her senses were tuned in unison with this warm night.

An explosion of laughter, like a burst of fireworks, followed by a loud applause reached her from the house; it didn't stop her, nor did it slow her body from moving forward.

"Marcel?" She whispered at first. The maze was just a dark silhouette. "Marcel!" She called out loud. Then one more time.

Sudden, unexpected fear washed over her. Except for distant voices from the house there was silence around her. She was alone, cut away from everybody.

Gerda turned and started jogging towards the house.

A new burst of noise. This time it was true fireworks. She didn't stop to watch. She ran steadily up the hill until she entered the terrace. "Hurry to the front, miss! They are all there watching the fireworks!" said one of the waiters, taking away dirty glasses and small plates. Though breathless, Gerda took his advice and walked across the space, through the French door. She couldn't understand her fear down there in the garden anymore. *What was all that about? Stupid.*

He's down there in the maze now, waiting for her, while she's up here wasting time! She has to run back down to the maze.

Gerda put her glass in someone's hand, turned and__ there was Marcel!

Thigh on thigh, hip on hip, his arms around Helga's waist! Her Marcel, in a tight embrace! As if they were indivisible. It all happened so swiftly. Jealousy mixed with hate. Add champagne_ a dangerous cocktail for a young girl. In Gerda's scenario Helga just forfeited her life with Marcel.

Gerda's first reaction was to show Helga the note, scream at Marcel, tell them who she really is, to make a scandalous scene. Instead, she left the small piece of paper in her purse, and left.

In the taxi she cried silently. Her tears were hot, angry streams. This was not going to be the end. She always gets what she wants. *They'll see.* She looked in her compact mirror: Adrienne. She knows she can make him change his mind. She smiled through tears at her image. Her eye make-up was smudged. Her eyes looked larger. She must remember this.

Gerda and Adrianne," We'll show him!" She focused on her eyes. She tried to look into their depth. It was thrilling. The warm tingling wave of doubled energy. Exhilarating, empowering. This is just the beginning. She is no longer Gerda, the little girl! She stopped crying, and tapped more rouge on her lips.

Marcel's car, his new, low, moss green Lagonda, shot forward. Helga didn't even notice. The new review was a success. It was ticking like an old clockwork. Marcel loved the new repertory. That wasn't surprising. That's who he was; kind of a 'review' guy. Helga had a dilemma. She was bored. Bored with Vienna. Bored with operetta, with the new review_all of it. She was ready to try something new, as soon as possible. To make a move towards what she really wanted_ dramatic theatre.

Helga looked at Marcel's profile. He was handsome and exciting. Satisfied with himself.

Yes, egocentric. Recently she started realizing her dependence on him. It flashed in her mind that if she stays any longer with him, soon she won't have any strength to go. She was certain that if she stayed, she'd ruined what they had together. She'd lose all of it __ herself, all of her talent, her dreams, their. . . she was looking for the most fitting word__"Love affair!" she said out loud. The engine was roaring and Marcel's mind under the driving leather helmet was stuffed with speedometers and horsepower. He didn't register a thing.

They were leaving Vienna in speed that Marcel would have loved to talk about all evening if she let him. Night lights were mixing with stars as the Viennese landscape was spread on many levels. Helga was indifferent to the Danube basin and the hills rising from it. She had no feeling for the wide, now constrained, river Donnau, the Blue Danube from the famous Strauss's waltz. There was no other landscape she would adore more than the stage.

Her ideal globetrotting comprised entirely a long chain of her professional engagements.

All that nationalisctic nonsense rising around. She never felt any loyalty to a land. For Helga Hayden there was no more important fatherland than theatre.

That was a complex dilemma. And no one to ask. Or perhaps, she could tell Bruno. Papa Bruno. Her only male friend. She loved him for not trying to get to her bed, like everyone else.

"She goes like the wind!" Called Marcel over the roar of the engine. It was more to himself and to the night. Helga put her head on his shoulder and hollered, "Who goes?" It was a rhetorical question, the answer was obviously 'Lagonda!'

Marcel didn't turn his head. With full force that Helga felt as it shook her head, he shouted straight forward "My Helga!"

Late that night she was looking out the window to the vast garden of Marcel's home; she felt that she didn't want to belong here anymore. All of those servants, gardeners, valets, his crazy parties. Everything at the tip of his finger. She felt with sudden dark impatience that she had to leave him; his world, his crowd as quickly as it could be arranged.

Marcel and women. That never bothered her. She should have admitted that her easygoing attitude was based on what he once said: he wasn't planning to marry. Ever. *Perfect.* Helga thought. She was not the marrying type either. So there. She couldn't be bothered by his adventures. Nothing deep, no true love, nor a dangerous affair. That all belonged exclusively to her.

Naiveté of her youth made her honestly believe in this equilibrium. When she comes back, he will be here for her, always. That, she felt, was granted.

There was no one as important for Marcel as she was. It flattered her, excited her to the core. She liked to tease him, playing 'hard-to-get' sometimes. Just a few hours ago, he tossed his knife across the room, "I'd rather see you dead than with someone else!"

The reason behind it was a letter she didn't want him to see; a letter she received from abroad. He noticed her swift movement as she tucked it away. She saw it now; it was daring to repeat his *What was it?* Her playing naive took him over the edge. It was thrilling.

Helga woke up excited. Her mind was rushing abroad. That letter was good news.

Marcel woke up. "You are an early bird today. Something's wrong?"

Helga turned over her shoulder to see if the lines of embroidery in the back of her stockings were straight. "I have a voice lesson I forgot about."

Satisfied, she shook her hips; her dress fell back into the perfectly designed folds. She rewarded him with her morning brightness and went to kiss him.

Marcel bought the lie. She looked great, and she knew it.

Marcel was watching her from their large white bed. "I'll tell my new chauffeur to take you. Josef. You'll like him." He adored everything about Helga. "I have an architect coming here at ten." he explained, watching her from the fortress of eiderdown pillows.

He tried to spoil her beyond fantasy. His was this madness he'd decided not to fight. Since their first night. It was a sheer deep obsession.

He didn't even mind that she had been playing with him, allowing other men to invite her to lunch. "Nice dress."

Helga smiled and made a line of dance steps. Her dress moved with her body in perfect harmony. White and red; latest fashion from Vionet. He bought it for her in Paris a few months ago. In his scenario a happy ending meant that he and Helga would drive into the sunset in his brand new car, and off to their life together.

Helga's escalating need for change was creating loud white noise. She wasn't capable, nor willing, to recognize any type of danger had it suddenly appeared. But she wasn't aware of that handicap, and rushed blindly forward.

Helga couldn't remember the last time she was this nervous. The stories about Max Steinhardt, especially his ways of auditioning actresses, were famous. She wasn't ready for him to say things like, "Hot air, miss, nothing but hot air is coming from your mouth; where did you leave your emotions? You want to play it like this?"

But Helga's will was strong enough to leave all of that behind the door when she was invited in. She made one precaution though. It was her friend Bruno Gottlieb's idea. She wondered now if it was more for his own sake when he'd suggested "Why don't you use a different name?"

At first, she wasn't keen; she slept on it. The idea of a safety net calmed her down.

She walked into Max Steinhardt theatre as __ Dora Glück. When she stepped outside after several hours, she didn't know who she was.

Helga waved down a taxi. Her tears were unstoppable. They were spoiling her new silk dress. She'd never been so intimidated, so humiliated, so scrutinized in all of her theatre career! All stories about Steinhardt were correct. *He is a bastard! An egocentric bully! A charismatic son-of-a-bitch!*

"Miss, are you all right?" The fatherly taxi driver, holding the door open for her, was honestly concerned.

Helga looked in the man's tired face. He didn't deserve this. Her face lit up. She said quietly,

"I am with Max Steinhardt" and then suddenly spread her arms and shouted

"I got it! I'm going to Berlin!" and hopped in the taxi.

Pressed in the corner of the backseat Helga felt cosy and free. There was sweetness in that. Helga exhaled. She was watching Vienna rushing outside the taxi window like a small cinema; she could hardly believe the journey she'd been on these past few years. A quick succession of vignettes: Her first meeting with Bruno . . . her audition for him . . . her first performance!

Bruno's "Who's next?" hollered through the open door. A short, stout man in his fifties. He touched the bridge of the bone frame of his spectacles, pushed it towards his forehead with his left index finger. His secretary, Miss Schlegel, guided in the next girl. "Miss Helga."

A young, petite, dark-haired woman slipped inside the office and smiled.

Her perfume, which meandered behind her, was obviously genuinely French. Bruno glanced at 'MissHelga' and all was clear to him. One of the rich girls had arrived to secretly join the theatre out of boredom. He was too tired to be polite. "Thank you! Next!"

But the girl didn't budge. She prepared a solo, and was here to show it to him.

She spoke, moved, sang, and did a few technically challenging dance steps. She was fun, musical and intelligent.

Bruno Gottlieb—an experienced, middle aged man, an artist in his own right, but a businessman in the first place— saw her potential. *She's got it!*

Helga knew that this theatre was an operetta, not a dramatic company. She didn't intend to stay here forever. She had chosen to start here. Just to get her feet wet in the novel theatre world. With naivete and arrogance of youth she said it all out loud.

Bruno's eyes behind his spectacles changed from shocked *What?* to amused loud "Welcome aboard!"

Bruno Gottlieb's Old Theatre surely had charm. It had Genius Loci. Perhaps, this was all she really needed. The little upholstered corner ceased being cozy.

"The Old Theatre!" Announced the taxi driver. "Pardon me, miss, who is that Max. . . somebody?" Helga handed the taxi driver several bank notes, and said with clear diction:

"He's the God of modern theatre!"

She was gone by the time the driver counted the money. She overpaid him like no one ever before. He pushed the "Vacant" sign down and headed home.

The morning light was coming into the bedroom through thin cotton drapes the color of raw silk. Gerda decided to keep her Adrianne disguise for as long as it was possible. It was a fun, exciting game. Getting harder to maintain minute after minute. This morning was like no other ever before.

Her eyes closed, she was aware of her naked body, for the first time in her life in a new, overwhelming way. The burning wound was making her prouder every second. There was no blood last night, just lots of dull pain. She tried to escape it when it became sharp. Then something happened and the feeling of belonging to her lover, the power she felt she had over him as he lost himself in the moment . . . it was beyond her dreams. Afterwards, her never before known fullness; as if her body used to be just a void until that very point.

Now, filled up to the brim with surprising contentedness, Gerda lost herself, her will, her past, her future. She was ready to follow the man sleeping naked next to her wherever he would choose.

The long, well-proportioned body stirred. Gerda smiled before he opened his eyes. She whispered almost inaudibly, "Good morning." It was the question of a little girl, not the greeting of a lover.

"Well, hello there." Marcel sniffled and hunched his back. He looked at her with one eye only, then closed it shut. He yawned, stretching his well-built arms above his widely opened mouth. He made such a loud sound; it almost broke Gerda's illusion of her romantic hero. Then he closed his mouth again and let the extra air pass through his nose. He stretched his arms and pulled his new lover next to him.

She didn't want to do anything that would make her seem disagreeable. She cuddled into the warmth and the sweet, pungent scent of his armpit.

"I am the happiest man in the world," he murmured, and fell back asleep.

"I am the happiest woman in the world," she said out loud, knowing that only she could hear it. The happiness of the last hours kept coming in waves she wasn't able to stop, even if she had decided to do so. She swept all her pain and discomfort to the periphery of this morning. Here was her new life. Now she belonged to Marcel. She felt incandescent happiness.

Marcel suddenly sat up. Gerda looked at his silhouette then pushed up her naked body and kissed the curve of his warm ribcage.

"You tickle!" His body moved from her reach. He dropped his legs from the high bed, and, stark naked, jumped down.

The morning sun was higher now and Marcel entered the patio. She watched him water his plants—vines, almost exclusively—then put the blue enameled jug back on a wooden shelf. He looked at her and winked. Freely moving in the nude, well-aware of the young woman's eyes following him through this morning. Gerda was shy to openly watch; she bent her head but her eyes couldn't have enough of his image. He enjoyed himself even more because of that.

He reached for his blue black-striped Turkish bathrobe, tightened the sash around his waist. He excused himself and walked round the wall; no door there to the adjacent bathroom; the familiar noises made Gerda blush. Then she heard him gargle water, his manly spits. His head appeared horizontally in the doorway. Toothbrush in the corner of his mouth, toothpaste foam balancing dangerously on his full lips, he asked with a funny lisp. "Breakfast?"

Gerda giggled and stretched her long, heavy-boned, blonde body. She felt girly, fragile, almost petite. "Yes! I am hungry," then she dared, "You made me hungry."

Her smile was so large that she was afraid it would never be able to fold back. It affected all of her words, her thoughts, her observations. Her mind stayed in place where it seemed to be existing apart from her. Sheer bliss! Everything she was feeling, everything she was saying felt brand new. She closed her eyes and must have slipped into a deep dreamless nap. The noise of a closing door woke her up.

Marcel brought a pot of coffee, cups, and slices of ham with fresh rolls. She watched him put one slice impatiently in his mouth. Like a boy, she thought, feeling warmth forming deeply inside her. Gerda imagined their children. The boys will be blonde like her, with a bronze complexion, and the girls will have Marcel's charm and curly hair . . . She reached for the coffee pot to cement the role of a mother, that she so profoundly felt at this moment, and poured.

Gerda was burning to tell Marcel her secret. But she found unexpected freedom and confidence in her new identity. She'll tell him later.

He handed her the bright coral cup of the finest, translucent porcelain. She started pouring and watched the golden lining vanish under the black liquid. Marcel bit into the crunchy roll. The whole ritual seemed so smooth, they both looked comfortable. *Like a long-married couple.*

It was as if this was a piece of choreography, rehearsed and performed seamlessly over many decades. She knew that they were meant to be forever. She's known that since she was a girl.

Marcel sipped from his coffee, smiled at her, kissed her lips that had just begun reaching for the brim of her coral and gold cup, and said softly and gently "You know, Adrianne, this is not going to work, right? You and I."

Gerda wanted to fix the rouge on her lips. She decided to smoke instead. She pulled the small golden cigarette case attached to a chain on her wrist, took out one of the thin, dark-brown cigarettes. There, in the glove compartment was the silver vesta, the one she stole from Marcel as a little girl. Her hands were trembling out of control. She can't smoke now.

Better to calm down first. The new lynx fur coat pulled close to her athletic body should help. A blond curl disconnected from her carefully coiffed hairdo. It swung in front of her blackened eyelashes and stayed there. She left it like that. She felt exhausted from her quick exit from Marcel's house, hours of frantic packing in her place. She changed her mind and took out Marcel's silver vesta, the one he gave her when she was a little girl. His cipher was engraved on top, encircled by laurel leaves. She will have hers next to his if she has to. . . A dark thought flashed inside the dyed pale blond head. She'd do anything for having him back. Anything. She knew it today.

She dropped the cigarette from absentminded fingers. She didn't bend to pick it up. The tip of her bespoke shoe twisted the rest of the sparks out of it. She looked at the blond tobacco smashed by her shoe. *He'll pay for this! He has no idea what deep hate women can feel.* She envisioned the whole process as if observing an anatomy class: Her hate as a dye coming from deep dark depths. It was spreading through her bloodstream to every vein, every vessel . . .

Gerda started tearing up. *Why? Why do I hate him with such force? Why did he bring out the worst in me?* It was not a cleansing cry after which one wipes her eyes and smiles towards a new day. This was a deep, angry sorrow mixed with bitterness. A helpless, silent cry tearing her throat. Love and hate.

Then there was a sudden change. Irrational. Dangerously simple. Uncalculated. Stemming from a very vague thought. Her tears stopped, and nerves calmed down.

She carefully wiped her nose, tapped dry the wetness from under her eyes.

Marcel belongs to her. Only her! For always. She saw a new avenue towards her dream. He simply forgot. It's not his fault. She knows now how to remind him.

Her brand-new little sports car slowly backed out onto the asphalt road. Gerda pushed the clutch to the first gear, and her new shiny toy shot forward.

Bruno refilled glasses and smacked "Mwah! That was a good year for merlot." He lifted the simple, thick, cast glass and examined the almandine color through the clear vessel. Then he picked up the bottle and looked at the label "I must send for more."

"Let's not tell anybody about my going to Steinhardt . . . yet . . . please." Helga looked at Bruno. He was with her on that. "No, of course not, dearie. I should order more of this."

Her eyes were not exactly focused after she sipped from the new glass,

"Thanks. Mm . . . yes you should. You are right, Bruno. It's better after it sits a little and opens up . . . Let's not announce it until I am safely in a running play in Berlin."

"I agree, child."

"Oh, Bruno . . . you've been so kind to me. Always. How will I ever repay you?"

"Once you are world-famous, come back as a guest star. You can tell the journalists about all of this then." He smiled at a sudden inner glimpse of her fame. "You'll go far, girl!"

"Thank you." Helga hugged him with uncomplicated warmth. "Let's not tell Marcel."

"You sure that's wise? What if Zelda told Jacob? What if everybody knows already?"

"I have my reasons."

"You know best."

"Saturday, then . . . How did she take it?"

Bruno, the director, chuckled "The Zelda-way! She worries about her stage fright. Silly. It never shows." And they laughed.

"Zelda will be fine. She has talent." He added her to the list of his 'racing horses'.

"She just needs to be told by someone, often." Helga pushed her empty wine glass forward.

"It's such a bummer"—Bruno carefully poured wine into the simple glass—"that Jacob Holzknecht decided to leave the theatre." He wiped the triplets of red drops on his desk. "They are quite a couple! We'll see how long they last."

Helga had a light buzz going. She shook her head. "They will. He's not the obsessive type."

Bruno looked at her over his glass. *Where did this come from?* But this wine was too good to spoil by philosophies.

"I will stay until the end of the show on Saturday, not to worry, Bruno. I'll travel on the Night Express."

"I knew you were a trooper! Thanks, my dear." He raised the glass in her honor. "You are a mensch, you know." Helga knew she shouldn't, but sipped from one more glass. "Where is Jacob going next?"

"That you won't believe."

"Try me." She finished her wine and pushed her glass towards her friend for a refill "This merlot grows on you."

"Jacob Holzknecht__wants to be a detective!"

"I never!" Helga's hand almost spilled the wine "Although . . . you know, Bruno, he's an honest guy."

"Yeah. . ." Bruno's speech was soaked in wine ". . . he's got a point there. When you look at it. . . detective's work must also be . . . a finely. . . finely balanced acting . . . at times . . . if you think about it."

ACT V

————— ⁓⁓✦⁓⁓ —————

Paternoster was the type of elevator which Helga particularly didn't like. It was the image of it, completely false, that someone gave her as a little girl: The open cabins, one above the other, moving in a chain which never stops, will go beyond the last floor, and there_ flip over!

She knew by now that it wasn't so, but her stomach had ignored the facts. She was frightened for a lifetime, expecting every time to fall on her head if she missed the chance to get out on time. *Oh, how stupid.* She was looking down at the tips of her beautiful pointy, grey Italian leather heels. They were polished to mirror shine. The small tortoiseshell buckles were round, like a small seal on this pact of elegance.

There were two more floors until the lingerie department. The open booth of the lift, that never stopped, was about to leave another floor. Helga noticed that the elevator was moving a bit quicker today. Would it be possible? She thought of the danger of missing the chance to exit when, in one large movement, a customer stepped up.

Helga looked at the familiar face "Jacob Holzknecht!"

"Helga!" He was genuinely glad to see her. He took off his fedora hat, "I thought you were leaving?"

"How do you know?" Then she understood. "Zelli. Of course."

"Nobody else knows, trust me. She's great at keeping secrets."

"Yes." They both chuckled, each for a different reason. "But I won't leave till after her show." She looked at Jacob, "I hope she knows that."

"That's great, thanks." *She's beaming!* Jacob observed Helga; it must have been the best mood he'd seen her in ages. "Are you going up?"

"I sure hope so." She started laughing.

"You'll go far with your extraordinary talent." Jacob got her joke.

"Thanks, Jacob. Yes, up. I'm going up to the lingerie." She giggled. He wished he had time to invite her for coffee. But he was busy.

"I'm meeting someone . . . along the line of my new work."

"Oh, on the last, unmarked floor?"

How does she know about that!? They shook hands and he gallantly helped her out when her floor came. *She seemed truly thankful.* Jacob, the detective, observed.

Jacob was glad he'd met Helga. He loved talking about Zelli.

The elevator was moving quickly. He should focus on his meeting. He'll be forever thankful to the old detective, Antonin; "Jacob, you are quicker and smarter than all of us here, together."

Great chap. "Go! Leave! Start your own agency!" The job here today was, in fact, thanks to him.

Last floor. Jacob was ready. He didn't like Paternoster elevators. Like a metaphor of an unsettled life. The open cabins, dangerous, one above the other, moving in relentless speed allowing at best for one step out. All day long, never-ending never-stopping chain of compartments. Someone told him when he was a boy that if you missed to get out before the last floor, the cabin flipped over. It scared him for life. Jacob's leg reached high for the down coming floor. The illusion was confusing. He stepped up. *Too soon!* Pain in his thigh was excruciating. He had barely enough strength to stand up. *Such Nonsense about falling on one's head!*

His hand touched the side of his jacket. The gun gave him confidence. He put the hat on and walked into his meeting.

The voices in the Imperial Greenhouse were muffled. It was a sanctuary of exotic plants. People behaved here the way they would in a church. Perhaps the similar height made them. The space was the antithesis of any church: full of light, airy, all glass and thousands of species of flora.

Drops of condensation kept falling in an unpredictable rhythm around Zelda. Her patience was running out. Her forehead became glossy with sweat; it wasn't because of the greenhouse. *Finally!*

"Where have you been?" Zelda turned her wristwatch face towards Franz Hirsch. She didn't try to hide how very vexed she was with him.

"Calm down. Hysterics won't take you far."

She had to be careful not to make him angry and leave. Her tone changed to a plea.

"This is my most important day."

"Just calm down." He glanced carefully around "First, give me my money."

Zelda saved "for costumes" just enough. It was not easy. She had to lie to Jacob. Her hand trembled ."Here."

She handed him rolled banknotes the way one rids himself of something dirty.

Franz took them with obvious skill. He knew he could trust her. She wouldn't dare trick him. He reached into his breast pocket. The small, white envelope was enforced by a wide, brown tape. Zelda grabbed it from him and stepped back. He shook his head, "You, of all people."

"Take your pity and shove it. . ."

"Whoa! Miss Zinger. Watch your language."

"What's it to you? Get out of here or I'll call the guard."

"You are mad," concluded Franz and turned to go away. After only a few steps he stopped, and turned around."I will say this—and it's only because I've known you so well—You don't need this."

"You don't understand, do you?" As if she was gnawing the words she was getting angrier. But Franz Hirsch was not easily pushed away,"I know theatre better than you do."

"You know nothing! This is my first big chance and I am not going to blow it because of my nerves!" Her muffled shouts turned so intense that he saw no prospect to reason with her now.

"I have talent! I must show them!"

Zelda's burning eyes full of tears made him retreat. He was now backing up, step by step,

"Show them then, Zelli, show them."

With a swift turn Franz started quickly towards the entrance. He felt a thirst for something strong. *Zelda! Stupid girl.* He always had a little bit of a crush on her. His fine hands, capable of making the best cut suits in Vienna, turned up the collar of his light jacket. Deeply angered, he rushed away towards the first beer tap he knew in the vicinity.

Under the lush canopy Zelda looked smaller and felt even more miniscule; her heart was pounding. Franz. Good riddance. She kept glancing around, her hands were cold.

The tremble didn't go away. She was prepared to do anything to have success. It was harder than she imagined.

Zelda picked up speed. The Imperial Greenhouse, her favorite retreat, ceased being the safe friendly spot she had created .

She was certain of one thing: Jacob would disagree. It would be the end of them. She knew by now that he wasn't obsessed with theatre the way she was. *He doesn't understand. She has a chance to have a breakthrough. Nobody can stop her now!*

Zelda thought of the envelope in her purse. She will take just a little, not to get hooked. She lifted the leather shell-shaped handbag on her chest.

The loud, harsh squealing of tram breaks startled her. She jumped to the side. Her heart was pounding inside her chest like when the conductor lifts his baton before the first tone of her aria.

It needed a moment to find its place. Here was the proof. A sign that she needed a little help. It's only for today; and, maybe, the next performance . . . just a little. After that she'll be famous and won't need any little crutch . . . like cocaine . . . ever again.

The backstage was still empty. Zelda walked to her new dressing room. Helga's dressing lady who came with it, was already finishing pressing Zelda's costume's bodice for the second act. "Excited?" She asked with a motherly smile.

Zelda liked her. "Ecstatic!" One look at her costume, a wave of stage fright weakened her thighs. "I think I will dress now for the first act . . . and take a little walk through the stage."

"Good idea, miss." Her dresser stopped ironing and brought Zelda's costume. It was much lighter than the other ones she'll wear for the second and third acts.

Zelda realized the difference in their weight when she started rehearsing in them. Only then she understood how challenging it was to dance and sing in such a colossal gown. She had to admire Helga for that. Zelda's stage fright moved to her stomach. *No, I can't be ill now!*

"You should put your wig on." Helga's voice chimed behind her.

"Oh, Helga!" Zelli stood up to greet her admirable colleague.

"I'm just stopping by to wish you luck . . . and to spit on you, toi toi toi!" Helga took Zelli in her arms and performed the little magic of theatre superstitions. She produced all the important spits ending with the loud "Break a leg!" and a suggestion of a kick toward Zelda's butt.

Zelda was beaming but her uncertainty already planted a small seed of doubt. "Superstitions have to be believed for them to work." She heard her grandma say. It was too late to regret all the questions she never asked her vaudevillian star grandma. It wasn't too late to declare defeat. She held Helga's hands in her small cold palms. Maybe, she could ask Helga.

"Look at you!" Helga was taking Zelda's arm and spun her slowly. "This is amazing! I've never noticed how similar we look!"

"It's so nice that you came." It was obviously too late for everything.

"I think nobody will see through our little trick . . ." Helga looked at the dresser. She made a simple my-lips-are-sealed mime. Their giggles filled up the room with camaraderie.

Helga helped Zelda fix her tall white wig. Done. She looked over Zelda's shoulder to the mirror. She was satisfied. "There is our new star!" She pressed Zelda's shoulders with enthusiasm and generosity which the dresser had never seen at Helga before. "Do you need anything more from me? I'll stay around."

"No, thanks. I must walk on the stage. . . alone."

"Why of course! My friends told me yesterday that my face was barely visible from the upper levels! I'll check it out." Helga blew her an air kiss and walked out of her dressing-room, which was now Zelda's.

Delayed "Thank you!" made Helga smile. She understood. The upcoming star's mind is elsewhere. To her own surprise she didn't mean it one little bit sarcastically.

Helga felt nostalgic; her dressing-room, her costumes, her theatre . . . Without her noticing, this theatre had become her first true home. All that was now turning into history.

She walked through the side door to the house, which is, she realized, such a lovely, fitting name; then she headed upstairs. From the very top of the house, she looked around.

Red carpets, gold everywhere: boxes adorned by thick, heavily gilded stucco of acanthus leaves, bunches of musical instruments, Greek drama masks. The warm glow when the light hits the surfaces! The slightly bitter scent of beeswax, resin, stage dust. There was a string attaching her heart to all this . . . and it pulled, and it hurt.

Helga sat down in the red velvet upholstered seat in the middle of the last tier.

She looked on the stage. The festoon was fine. They fixed it.

She had an unexpected time to look around; to print into memory all the beauty, to take it away for her long trip late tonight.

The enormous chandelier in the middle was, at this hour, still a white and gold blossom waiting in the quiet of dawn. Its stem was surrounded by a gilded disc of overlapping acanthus leaves. When lit, it shimmers and glissens under the large colorful circle of the nine Muses.

The sound of an oboe came from the orchestra pit. The same eight tones again, and again. Some false notes from last night had to be fixed. Helga smiled. Sounds of home.

Her face was wet. Has she been silently weeping for . . . how long?

She never wept for Marcel. Looks like she never will. It was a strange feeling running away from him. He made it clear over and over again that in his mind she belonged to him. Flattering as it was, there was a golden cage in the making. Recently, he would say things like" You are mine, You belong to me, I need only you," completely unexpectedly in the most extreme moments. In between their kisses, in the wings before she ran on stage, and more and more often during their sex. Their love-making. . . her hesitation brought up a pressing question. What was it, indeed?

It's been intense; as exciting as ever. She enjoyed his jealousy too much. She feared it too. It felt like being on Paternoster. No. She won't stay until the last floor.

She was right not to tell him.

Marcel was looking across the vast space of his ancestral land. His manicured fingers struck a match on the ribbon of the small silver vesta. His left hand immediately crouched to shield his cigarette from the lake breeze. He took a draft and exhaled, rubbing the rectangular silver body with a tobacco-stained thumb. He had his coat-of-arms chiseled into it. He looked at it.

He didn't have any enthusiasm for his family motto. He omitted to have it engraved there. Vincit Veritas, Truth Conquers. In his line of business creativity was above truth. His sentiments were clear. No, he did not have the ambition to stay in his family seat, nor to propagate his family's three-hundred-year-old bloodline. His brothers were already doing that. He came here because his father was fading away.

Marcel was the youngest. His mother's baby. He looked nothing like his father. Early on it occurred to him how different he was. He loved numbers. More than anything. More than hunting. More than boating on the lake. More than horses. He loved numbers in their most exciting state__ money.

Here he was. Overlooking the lake, park, gardens, the forests on the surrounding hillsides.

He felt no connection.

Back in the house his father was living the last days of his life, and all that Marcel had left in him was anger. He wished he'd taken Helga with him here. Would his brothers be furious?

He thought so. But then. . . What does he know about them? Less than what he's able to put together about Helga's new plan.

They are countrymen, hunters, farmers. It's better that he left Helga behind, in Vienna. He saw it clearly now.

Helga wants to be a 'serious actress.' Marcel wasn't sure what that meant exactly. For him, anyway. His knowledge of theatre was focused on light genres. He was never patient with someone's deep emotions; on the stage or off.

Serious actress. Big words, grand gestures, intellectual debates analyzing someone's writing. Looking for more emotions. New engagements, new leading men. Jealousy made him toss his cigarette, he immediately lit the next. Of course there was that rumor. Marcel couldn't think he'd ever heard the name Steinhardt before. He could ask her. Would she tell him the truth? The rumor about her audition must have been just that_ a rumor.

Helga Hayden. She was worth all his money. Never before he met this petite, uninhibited little nymph had he been completely obsessed with a girl.

Marcel extinguished the cigarette in his fingertips. He was not afraid of pain. His father respected that. Marcel hurriedly walked inside the house and went straight to the phone. Then he looked at his new 'tank' wristwatch, and hung up. Helga had probably started preparing for her performance. Monumental wave of irrational jealousy had swept through him.

His car was ready. He'll step on it.

Helga was still sitting in the gold and crimson of the upper balcony when she heard her name called from somewhere down underneath. It was not for at least an hour and a half before the doors open to the audience. The voice was her dresser. Helga waved at her. "Up here!"

The sound filled up the tall gilded space "Helga, you have a message!" She waved a piece of white paper.

"I'm coming down!" The acoustics of this house were perfect. Helga was down in no time. "Here. The dresser handed her a small folded piece of paper. "A messenger gave it to the stage manager."

"A messenger? Who is it from?"

The old dresser's eyebrows raised up in silent 'who do you think?' said it all. "__Marcel."

"Marcel?"

Helga's reaction confused her dresser. She thought she knew those two more than well. Helga's panic stricken mind was busy. So this was his surprise. She'll have to tell him the truth now.

"How are you feeling?" Helga noticed Zelda walking around, off stage, repeating lines of her text. "Are you all right?"

"I'm fine." Zelda tried to control her voice. "I think. . . I feel like. . . I'm coming down with something."

"Nonsense. You look great. It's nothing." Helga's voice was a command. *She's not going to panic and make me go on stage in her place? Is she? No. Not going to happen!*

"Zelli, it's nothing. Look at you! All is perfect; your costume, your wig . . ." Helga's cajoling seemed to be working better.

"I'll just walk some more." Zelda's voice sounded a few notches calmer.

"You look fantastic!" was a team effort. Helga and her dresser looked at each other. "Poor thing. She seems nervous." It was unclear if Zelli heard that.

Helga opened the note. Of course, typical Marcel: "I need to kiss you now, in the maze."

In a hurry, as always. She shouldn't have lied to him about Steinhardt. The die was cast.

What can happen? He'll be mad at me. Not the first time, not the last. That's all. Helga convinced herself that Marcel would understand that this is the best for her at the moment.

He's a risk-taker himself. Perhaps, he'll come and join her in Berlin. There! That's it. He'll like the idea. Helga looked again at Marcel's note. "I have to kiss you. . ." Pleased with her conclusions, she shook her head. Notes, promises; the most incredible nights and days in his luxurious sheets . . . She would have sworn that his intuition must have warned him. How could it not? He's an experienced man. He's a player. They are.

Helga knew that there would never be anything as perfect as what she's had with Marcel. They were born for each other. He was crazy about her. Her smile widened. *All right then! One last time.*

Although Helga wasn't keen on that place. *Fear. How silly!* He should have his wish. Especially tonight. She ran her fingers through her freshly permed hair, *The Maze it is, just for Marcel.*

Zelda made up her mind. She tried to do it on her own. She walked on stage, around it repeating her lines to calm down her nerves. She gathered all her willpower_it failed her. She was walking among the shrubs in the atrium. She knew well about the obscured side door. It takes you on the staircase leading down to the Maze. She'll be safe down there.

Her steps quickened propelled by her growing inner tremble. She took her wide, pink skirts to pinch and walked downstairs. She couldn't hurry as fast as she had planned in her costume; the volume of both her skirts and her wig was weighing her down. Last few steps. She looked around the underground space. It was sparsely lit. Perfect. There was a concealed spot by the back wall.

She'll be safer over there.

The outline of the old scenery looked like a graveyard... No! She must not do this to herself . . . It looked like _a gypsy camp in the dusk. Yes. Zelda's nose registered the smell of dry paint and resin preserved from the old productions, the theatre stage. On the cue her stage fright returned. Zelda pulled out the envelope from her neckline. Her hands were shaking again. With the utmost effort she carefully undid the tape. Now she had to wait before her fingers were capable of holding still.

She remembered what Franz told her to do; she ripped part of the paper, made a fold, then poured a little bit of the strange white powder in it. She hesitated but a new wave of fright pushed her. She took a sniff and waited a bit. Nothing happened. Did Franz trick her? Did he sell her talc powder instead of the real thing? To save her? Zelda felt more desperate than angry. She poured a larger amount into the fold than before.

Helga heard a slight, remote noise from the Maze just like the other time. Her steps slowed down. The afternoon light was still sufficiently coming through small, narrow horizontal windows in the stair shaft. She stepped forward carefully. Her face started changing as if she put on a new makeup. Pink with blush. Her excitement was palpable. She heard the quiet movements from underneath. Marcel was already waiting__Blankets, pillows and champagne. He knows how to seduce. She was drunk on excitement. Helga couldn't wait for the surprising moment when she appears from nowhere. She had to focus very hard now. Her plan comprised walking quietly on her tiptoes up to her lover and then__

Helga made a quick retreat sideways into the shadow. She didn't know what to do!

There, in front of her, was Zelda, sniffing cocaine. It was surreal!

Zelli truly looked like Helga herself in that costume and that wig. Helga noticed once again today that she was built absolutely identically. Helga's brain was speeding through this unexpected dilemma. Where is Marcel? She must stop him!

No, she should stop Zelda first. Talk to her? What then?

Uncertain, Helga hesitated__ then froze in the dark.

The tall figure of Marcel, his hat on, appeared from nowhere.

It all happened as if behind a bobbinet screen. Helga stood there petrified.

She heard a strange flat sound, sort of a smack; then Zelda's body slowly folded forward towards the back wall and dropped to the ground.

Helga's hands shot up to her mouth. She pressed her lips sealing the scream inside her throat. Her brain was at its highest speed: Don't scream! Don't move! Don't panic! She was mortified. Paralyzed with fear. She was watching her own murder! One more 'smack'. *A gun with a silencer.*

Then the murderer turned and rushed out as quickly as he walked in, his coat almost brushing Helga standing in the shadow.

In the sudden silence Helga's heart threatened to shatter her eardrums. She was shaking, unable to think. In stupor, without strength to move. When finally her instincts kicked in she rushed forward to save Zelli. But the shots from close range were too exact. Zelda's body in Helga's costume, red blood spot on its back, was without life.

Helga started slowly backing up. Her mind was too overworked, too shaken for any plan.

She almost tripped over a small object. It slipped a few inches further. Helga picked it up and put it immediately in her pocket. She was stunned at first to even process what had just happened . But then, her hand in the pocket knew. Marcel's silver vesta, the match-box with his initials was in her palm now. Safe.

So, he'd heard . . . he didn't want any explanation. Helga started turning the facts from all sides. Her brain was rushing forward. She could hardly keep up.

She must forget everything that she just witnessed. She must make herself go and find him. Tell him everything. Help him escape. The possibility of Marcel being hunted down was unbearable! *They'd find and hang him!* She started walking away as quickly and as quietly as possible. She pictured him in his sports car driving away through the meandering streets of Vienna. *Go! Speed up! Quick! Hurry away!* As she stepped back in the garden she heard the orchestra through the open door.

The show! It suddenly occurred to her that there's no one else to do it but her.

Her legs began rushing forward. Here was something she knew how to handle.

She started speeding across the lawn. A window was pushed open at the director's office.

"Helga! Thank God . . . Come in immediately!"

Bruno caught her in the stairway. "Have you seen Zelda?"

"Yes. No."

"I can't find her."

"Aha." Helga was like a mechanical toy, but Bruno was too concerned about his show to notice.

They rushed towards the stage; he tried for the last time: "Zelda!"

Helga couldn't make herself tell him the truth now; she wanted to say 'she's not here' but that would have endangered Marcel. She knew what she had to do now.

They heard the audience filling up the auditorium, the instruments in the orchestra in their solitary warm-ups before the first violin comes in to give them the C note. Bruno turned towards Helga. Before he could speak, she said: "Yes!" and started running towards her dressing room.

Several hours later Helga's friend, the theatre director, Bruno Gottlieb, was certain that this was the most peculiar performance Helga had ever given. She was like an automatic doll! It was obvious that her mind was already in Berlin. She didn't even stop to say Goodbye. Bruno was hurt.

Helga, her performance over, rushed to the stage-door and out. Her plan was clear. She'll get in the taxi waiting for her and go home to pack and off to . . . Her blood turned into a block of ice — there was Marcel, sitting in his sports car parked next to her taxi. She stopped for a second but it was long enough for him to register her familiar movement. She caught his eyes.

Eyes of a murderer! Now she saw it. His look was wild and didn't leave any doubts. He must have realized his mistake and waited here to correct it. *He has the gun!*

Her panic was instant, catapulting her into an almost air-born turn. Her need to save him fell through.

Helga rushed up the short staircase around the theatre concierge. She flew through the backstage and through the side door, up the red carpeted aisles that muffled her heels working the steep elevation. She mixed with the crowd of audience in the vestibule. Somebody recognized her and people tried to circle her. Some of them were applauding. Her hope that nobody would recognize her was a wish of a little child under a napkin playing invisible. She gave smiles all around trying not to break her speed.

Once out the gilded front door she flew down the red granite steps. She turned right and rushed to the taxi stand. She hopped in the first empty taxi she saw. "Hauptbahnhof! Bitte . . . fast!"

The taxi driver knew that command too well. If there's a train to catch, he knows shortcuts to the Main Station like no one in this town.

High above passengers' heads a sleepy, monotone nasal voice kept announcing: "Vienna Hauptbahnhof! On the fourth platform the express train from . . . just arrived . . . On the seventh platform the Orient Express is leaving . . . finish boarding to . . . Paris express on platform three!" Booming in high pitch over the crowds, echoing through the vast glass and cast-iron space it was hard to understand. Shouts of people on the ground were coming from different directions. A busy station like this one never sleeps.

In the taxi it came to Helga that her suitcases were still standing in the hallway in her apartment. She fished a few coins and found a telephone booth. Her fingers were shaking as she dialed the operator. She wished it could go straight through. Finally! Her housekeeper will send her luggage to Berlin Bahnhof and _of course _not a word, to anybody. Helga heard herself talking but she couldn't recognize her own voice.

She saw a young woman trying to pick-pocket a robust gentleman. Helga would have normally yelled, but this was not her moment. She watched as the girl, not being skillful enough, failed her attempt. The man was still strolling with his golden watch safely inside his pocket.

Helga glanced at that poor young woman's appearance. It occurred to her that by sheer luck, she didn't have to look like that. The young woman saw her. Helga looked straight at Bertha. They registered that instant in their memories before slipping back to their own incomparable reality.

In the next quick sequence Helga found the platform, paid a coin, showed her First Class ticket, and passed through the low tourniquet. Only then she was able to breathe.

The Berlin Night Express was ready for its long journey. "Your luggage, Madame?"

"No luggage," she said with a flair of a globe-trotter who has everything under control, who just indulged one of her spontaneous ideas to hop to another European Metropolis.

"Very well, Madame," said the wagon-lit concierge and, under his breath, added

"How did your performance go tonight?"

Helga turned to him. "Excuse me?"

"Pardon my impertinence, Miss Hayden, I am a fan, a great admirer."

Helga had a split second to make everything look perfectly normal. She focused all energy in it. Her voice lowered, she looked him in the eyes with a smoky glint.

"I'm, secretly, off to Berlin. Nobody knows but you and I, for now." She managed to wink at him.

He would have screamed out of joy. If only. Instead, he said as quietly as possible, "I understand . . . Not to worry, madame. I'll be discreet. Thank you for this!"

Out loud, he returned to his formal, "Follow me, please, madame. This way." He couldn't help but wink at her before he closed the sliding door of her compartment.

Her first-class coupé was a comfortable space, clean and pleasantly scented. Helga didn't notice that it was roomier than the first-class International Express from her trip to Vienna years ago. She tossed her small porte-monnaie on the pristine bed and reached for a glass of water.

She drank it in one gulp, filled it again from the prepared steel jug. This time she allowed more time. Cool liquid started calming her down. She looked around. The satin pajamas, neatly folded on top of her blanket, were in pale orange — her least favorite color. The hems were white, so it was "Just fine." Helga heard herself say.

She stepped into the chrome-and-black washroom. The space wasn't small at all. She didn't quite register any of it. Neither the shiny white sink, nor the almond scented little soap.

Everything was mechanical; as if someone was dictating her_ pour the water, unwrap the soap, wash your face! The towels were a bit rough, but Helga didn't feel it. She scrunched up the soap wrap and tossed it in the black porcelain bin.

She was still in a glass bubble. Her feelings, her senses stayed in the theatre in the Maze. She wasn't able to bring them on the stage tonight. She failed Bruno.

Her naked face in the rectangular mirror in front of her was without expression. Was this Helga? Without a trace of any make-up, her washed face was like nothing her fans were used to seeing. No, nobody would be able to recognize her.

There was the whistle, the slamming of doors announcing that she was about to leave all of her Viennese life behind. Helga laid down on the crisp bed just to have some rest, to close her tired eyes. To bring back feelings. Only that the film she started watching under her eyelids was too disturbing. In place of a newsreel was Marcel's "I'd rather see you dead than with someone else." There was the image of Marcel upset beyond everything she knew before;

Next, his note, her slow steps downstairs_ Zelli falling forward. . .

No, she can't sleep. An old saying came to her, *When you are with people, guard your words; when you are alone, guard your thoughts.* She needs to be among people.

The train started moving. She heard the tugging of heavy pistons, hissing puffs of steam, the train gave a series of short whistles, and off it started moving up north. Helga was getting closer to her new life on the famous Berlin stage. It felt like someone else's story. She felt nothing.

Helga stood up, brushed her skirt smooth, and tapped some perfume from a miniature flacon to her neck and on her wrists. She gave her cheeks several small pinches for a bit of color. She was ready to go to the dining car.

Negotiating the short, jerking movements as the train was crossing the braids of train tracks, her body was bouncing from side to side, she felt it as a dance; it cheered her up. She was finally waking up from her stupor.

"Life is just a bowl of cherries . . . don't take it serious . . . life's too mysterious." She could hear her favorite little song somewhere in front of her! She hurried up toward the comfort of music, the familiar sounds. She pushed the door open. The bright lit space was in full swing. "Will you dine with us, madame?"

". . . so live and laugh at it all!" The song ended on a high note. Helga said "Yes".

The engagement party at the Old Theatre was to be held backstage. Bruno Gottlieb, the director, agreed. What's more fun than a party in the theatre? It was going on and on_ all night long. The last day of the theatre season behind them, all the staff were ready to celebrate into the wee hours. Birds started singing in trees. The small park in the atrium was waking up. Repetitive sounds of giggles and nonsensical drunken, wannabe-serious-and-focused, slurping speeches preceded the loud couple of lovers cutting their passage through the underground maze.

"I need to pee," said the female voice.

"You don't mean it? Oh god . . . Hold it! Go back!"

"I can't . . . we drank too much . . . turn! I'll squat right here."

"You are a lady, you can't!"

The young woman laughed "I can do as I please . . . I have to! You turn!"

"Not here! Jeee-sus! Go over there!"

She stopped on the verge of darkness as if balancing on top of an abyss. "Here?"

"No, not there . . . go further . . . fur-ther."

The young woman moved her drunken existence unwillingly into the shadows.

Her companion turned, stumbled into the corner behind him, unbuttoned his fly, and relieved himself.

Fortissimo of her deafening scream seemed to have peeled off layers of the heavily whitewashed walls.

In a few moments, the two scared young people were looking on the floor. He was holding the lit match high above their heads. The body of a woman in an opulent costume, face down, was framed by a puddle of blood drying around its edge.

"Ouch!" The match reached its end and burnt his tobacco-tinted yellow fingers.

In the abrupt dark, the young woman leaned against him "It's Helga . . . all the blood! I think I'm going to..." She started sobbing.

"You are a woman. You can't. You are used to . . . all those things."

"Yeah, but I am going to puke anyway."

"No . . . you can't," said her boyfriend right before he started sliding to the ground.

"He fainted!" announced the young woman to the dark Maze.

ACT VI

Marcel entered the bar. Music was playing. "Life is just a Bowl of Cherries."

What an irony that is, he thought. He felt like everything had spilled out of his full bowl. Cherries turned sour. He looked at the bartender. "The usual!"

The young man stepped back and opened one of the three coolboxes. He didn't have to ask which champagne. This was Baron Van Getz; it had to be crème de la crème.

Marcel pulled the wide-open shallow champagne glass toward him. Maître d' registered his delayed movements. Marcel let it stand. The fine drink turned flat without him noticing.

"Will you be dining tonight, my lord?" The old maître d' came up to him.

"No. Thank you, Tomislav. I will stay here, at the bar."

"Pardon my impertinence, my lord, but is everything all right? We haven't seen you for quite some time."

"No, nothing's all right . . . nothing at all. But thank you for asking, Tomislav." With a slight bow the ever discreet old man left.

"Maybe something different, my lord?" The bartender pointed at the champagne glass.

"Yes. Give me something stronger, Joe, whiskey, perhaps . . . make it a double."

Marcel was in shock. *So it's over.* Jealousy clouded his whole day; anger eliminated any common sense. He was lost.

The heavy whisky-glass arrived_The amber liquid, chopped ice floating on top. Marcel took a swig.

It all happened so fast. Where did he make a mistake? It shouldn't have ended like that!

Helga was . . . He couldn't make himself finish the thought. The past tense was unbearable. He asked for more whiskey. Helga. There will never be one like her. What was he thinking? She had the 'Proustian wings' in her eyes. She had access to the secret scale of his body. To the halftones and brios, he would have never known otherwise. A conundrum he wouldn't let anyone else discover.

The ice cubes rattled in the new empty glass; then, more golden liquid filled up the void.

Neither the bartender nor maître d' had seen baron Van Getz drunk before. Professional experience dictated their moves_ polite and agreeable.

The wireless was playing the melody Bruno had used in his review. Marcel's face changed. The mood in the room seemed to follow. His eyes were smiling. He picked up the heavy glass and looked through the cut crystal ornaments. It sparkled within, giving out all colors of the spectrum. His idea was brilliant! It was short of a miracle. *A lifesaver*, he thought.

Enter_Adrianne! Slim, strong, young. Fresh and new. He'll go and buy an exquisite piece of jewelry. *Yes!* He'll do it first thing in the morning! He will send it to her in a bouquet on the stage tomorrow night. Marcel didn't touch the new full glass. He has to be in great form for tomorrow.

He's an athlete, after all. He recalled their unfinished encounter with relish. Marcel felt like embracing the whole of humanity.

The bartender looked at him, surprised by the sudden change. But then_that's what alcohol does to some people. *Fascinating!* Nothing he hasn't seen before. He turned and placed Marcel's glass in the steel sink. It joined other glasses under the constantly running stream of clean water. If only this were possible to do with some patrons.

Banknotes Marcel placed under the leather square coaster would have easily covered a night-long party.

He picked up his top hat and left.

"Next!" Called Bruno Gottlieb from the middle of the auditorium. *But who? That girl is hopeless.* His thoughts were unsettling. *Good chorus girl, total flop as a solo.* He gave her a try, as Helga had suggested. Helga was the best of them all, and now she's left. Thank God the theatre season is practically over. He was glad he hadn't advertised the new talent, because in the end_there was no talent at all yet. "What is it, Miss Schlegel?"

His secretary was standing on the side of the empty stage, fidgeting; "That was all, Bruno."

He gave a loud sigh. "Those girls . . . they come and go as a tide of glorious smiles and red lipstick. No Helga."

No Zelda either_ poor girl. That thought gave him shivers. The police were all over his theatre for days. Cocaine! What was she thinking! They concluded that whoever sold her the drug had killed her. They'd arrested one Percy . . . somebody . . . then let him go. No evidence.

It was only thanks to Bruno's long-standing good connections there was only a small notice about the death of an actress in the papers. No other press. *Lucky!* Another murder in the Old Theatre would have ruined him, he feared. He lit his cigarette for at least the third time today. Perhaps now he can step out in the garden and smoke it. He turned off the little lamp over his portable desk placed on top of the red velvet backrests.

Bruno felt about that audition what he felt when the horse he bet on lost. The cigarette in his lips he changed his mind and walked upstairs to Miss Schlegel's office"When you see Adrianne, tell her to stop by later."

"Yes, Mr. Gottlieb "She looked at him with admiration." Of course! With Helga gone, Adrianne is going straight to the top, isn't she? Lucky girl!" Tactful, as always, she didn't mention Zelda.

Bruno looked at her. *She's right!* He put Adrienne in a box with the label "Review" on it; perhaps she has more hidden talents; she might be a talented actress! Who knows.

The new season was safe. Pink and yellow filters slid in front of the lights of Bruno's day. All will be fine again. He went to his office and took out the slivovitz he had stored for "a special occasion." He poured himself a good measure and lifted the thick red glass to the smoke-saturated space. "New beginnings!" he called to his reflection in the tall bookcase glassdoor.

In a few moments, Miss Schlegel tactfully closed his door.

Gerda pulled over and parked in front of a sideroad café. She stepped up from her new, glossy yellow toy. The new Benz. Elegant and chic. She entered the establishment, ordered Viennese with double whipped cream *No Strudel, thank you.* The waitress noticed the fine suede accessories. *Beige. A dream!* Before the waitress could return, Gerda took down a newspaper stretched on a light rattan frame from the brass wall hanger.

She opened it on the last page. Theatre notices were very favorable. It was fun having all that success. But, it's all over for now!

She no longer exists in the Viennese theatre world, she's no longer Marcel's one-night stand: Adrianne is dead! Long live Gerda! She had such fun! She tricked them all! At least, she hoped she did. Her eyes had dark circles under them. She hasn't been sleeping well. Gerda looked out of the bay window over the blue lake. It was misty after the morning rain. White veils rolling on the water looked like shrouds. Gerda felt shivers throughout her body. *Stop it! Stupid.* She has more guts than all of them together. Her memory was not settling for her cheerleading. Shivers kept coming through her spine. Light tremble reached her fingertips. She waved to the waitress and ordered a thick slice of Strudel. The mist behind the large windows turned heavier, the 'shrouds' spread into one solid screen. She will have to drive slowly from here.

Gerda's sports car crossed the short bridge and stopped in the courtyard. Her father's new favorite place as of last year. He always wished for a little castle. *He gets what he wants.* Gerda's like him.

She waited for the valet to open the door for her. Her long, slim legs touched the freshly raked sand in unison. Under the elegant moss green skirt, she held her knees properly together. As she stepped out and stretched her arms above her head, the yellow leather driving helmet in her hand, she exclaimed. "Home!" Her smile was broad, warm. "Careful with my hat boxes!" She lifted her shoulder to secure the red fox shawl which was an elegant finishing touch to her 'hunting look'.

"Gerda!"

The name sounded so unfamiliar Gerda almost forgot to turn; she had been Adrienne for almost one whole theatre season. She was quick to conceal it. She tossed the driving helmet to the first valet. Her arms opened in a welcoming gesture towards_"Lotty!"

She smiled, now even more confused. "You're here. What's going on?"

She noticed the servants coming for her luggage were smiling knowingly. She glanced at her childhood friend "Where is everybody?"

Lotty's face was as pleasant as ever. *Is she blushing?*

"I wanted to talk to you before everybody else." Her arm stretched in front of Gerda, "Look!" She couldn't hold her joy back any longer. "Your brother proposed."

"Ah! What a lovely ring! Oh, Lotty! It's simply marvelous! Congratulations!"

Lotty observed her future sister-in-law. Frankly, she wasn't certain how Gerda would react. She's known her long enough.

"Upset?" Gerda reacted with sincere surprise to her friend's next confession. She took Lotty under her athletic arm. Her answer came spontaneously cheerful, her friendly squeeze was genuine.

"Why would I be upset?" Her rupture of energy, her 'There's luck for everyone! Wouldn't you say?' took Lotty by the most wonderful surprise.

"Yes! I believe it now." Lotty agreed. "But one must push it sometimes. Wouldn't you say?" She immediately regretted saying that. But it had no impact on Gerda in any way.

The whole family was there. They were coming down the narrow granite steps from the main wing. Those surprisingly tall men were Gerda's brothers. She couldn't take her eyes off them.

"And how was Vienna?"

"Papa! It was all Divine!"

She turned quickly to Lotty "'Push it a little,' you say? I'll think about it."

"Vienna was a dream; I will go back there as soon as it can be arranged."

"Arranged what?" Said Gerda's father, walking towards his only daughter. There was Mother. Smiling. Somewhat more tired than Gerda expected"Darling! How did you enjoy driving your new car? Papa insisted you needed a new one."

"She's our pride and joy. Of course she needs a new car!A diploma from the Viennese Conservatory of Music!"

"Brava!"

"Oh, Papa, I can't think of a better man!" exhaled Gerda, and meant it.

"I am ruined! Ruined!" Bruno Gottlieb's shouts boomed throughout his theatre. "What's happening? Who's doing this to me!" He sat down in his chair and looked at Miss Schlegel.

"We lost Adrianne!" he stretched his arm with Adrianne's letter, clasped in between his fingers, towards his shocked secretary. He wished his dear Hubert was here. He would never say late Hubert.

"Adrienne?" Miss Schlegel was puzzled. "But her notices were excellent!"

"I know. All of them. How often has that ever happened? Now, she's had something urgent to attend to. Imagine__urgent! What in the devil can be more urgent than theatre?" Bruno was beside himself. "Amateur! Dilettante! Irresponsible louse!"

This is what he gets for everything he's done for that long stick without talent! All right, she had talent.

"She could have been the new Maria Ziggler!" Such a lost chance was difficult to swallow. "They would have carried her home on their shoulders!" He recalled his student's years and the Divine Ziggler whose horses they would take out and pull her carriage in their place! Youth. No, today's young have no idea about true devotion to Art. Bruno was furiously devastated.

Miss Schlegel placed the letter on Bruno's desk in the slowest, most inconspicuous manner,

"I have some correspondence to attend to. . ." Ever tactful and discreet, she closed the door as she was leaving.

Against his good judgment, Bruno Gottlieb poured himself a stein full of slivovitz he got from his cousin in Moravia. He drank it Prosit! in one gulp. That was not a good idea.

He wanted to say something else but his tongue got heavy and twisted. His whole body became a nonfunctional, uncoordinated stranger, an unfeeling blob; his office swayed forward and then one more time back. His head became a cloud which got stuck between mountains . . . Bruno Gottlieb had to take an unprecedented nap.

Gerda's feet hurt from the high, narrow heels she wore all day yesterday, to show off. Low slippers were all she could fit in today. She sat down and hung her ankles across space on the edge of the low coffee table.

She leafed through the large pages of a fashion magazine. Jan, the valet, came in. His tactful 'cough' made her put her feet where they belong_on the floor. She stretched her legs on the carpet, without looking at him, and asked "May I have a drink?"

"Your mother is on the verandah, miss. She'd like a word."

Gerda's tall figure floated towards the open door. The jumper arrived from Paris yesterday. Pale blue silk becomes her. She glanced across the space to the garden terrace. The whole castle was in the last stages of preparations before the guests started to arrive.

Her mother was making last minute orders, changes in the seating and coordinating flower delivery with the photographer and the press. "Sit down, darling. I need to talk."

Gerda sat down across from her; the thinly upholstered loveseat wasn't comfortable but she stayed. "I am here, Mama." She said it with a transparent concern like when she was thirteen.

Gloria had a hard time not to smile. *What did she do this time?*

"I had hoped that you met someone interesting in Vienna, dear."

Gerda immediately thought __a trap. *What do they know?* She decided to tread carefully before ruining her prospect to return to Vienna. "I was under the impression that you and papa had a husband for me in mind."

"Yes, a husband. . . We thought about that. But for now, we disagree."

"Disagree about whom?"

"Nevermind. Until we are in accord about your future there's no reason to discuss it. Am I right?"

Gerda's jaw slipped forward. Her mother noticed. "You are not going to be cross with us, now? I thought you had more plans about returning to Vienna?"

"Well. . . I have. I'd like to take more lessons. With somebody famous."

"That could be arranged." Gloria wondered how serious her daughter is about opera. "Do you have anybody in mind?"

"Hermine Rosetti."

Gloria was surprised by the immediate exact answer. Pleasantly so. There was an interest.

"Have you spoken to her already?"

"I wouldn't dare before talking to you and Papa." That was a lie. Only her mother knew what Gerda could be capable of.

"You should, soon. I'd like to meet her. You see, I haven't been myself lately. My doctor says it's my nerves. Don't they always say that?"

"Mommy?"

The valet brought Gloria her afternoon sherry. She took it and held it without touching it. Gerda's face completely changed. Her annoyed attitude was gone, there was nothing mundane about her anymore either. As if her rediscovered fear washed her adult features back into a frightened little girl. "What's wrong, mommy? Does papa know?"

"Oh no! Let's not tell him; he loves us all strong and healthy."
Was there an irony?

Gloria picked up the caring tone "Oh no, really. He must not know." She sealed it with "Promise." It was a command. None of her usual slow suggestions, so easily disobeyed.

Another of their benign pacts was being made. "Close the door, darling. Come here."

She tapped the seat "Next to me."

Gerda did as her mother asked; once she was close to her, she noticed that under layers of powder, her mother's face looked tired and__old.

Gloria caught her fingers and held her softly without any effort.

"I heard you are a good actress. . ."

"Mommy, you knew?"

"How else would you be able to stay in Vienna, my little girl? For almost one full theatre season? You are a child."

"I am not a child."

"No, of course not. You are an artist. I am very proud of you, darling."

Gerda's throat was tight, her tears were making it impossible to say thank you.

Her mother gently patted her hand. "Now, darling. There's a story I'd love to hear from you." Gloria took a small sip of sherry, "You don't have a drink! What would you like?"

"I asked for a drink but it somehow never happened."

"Oh, I'm sorry. They are all so busy with your brother's engagement party." Her hand had just one massive ring on her left middle finger. She noticed Gerda looking at it. "That was my great-grand mother's."

Gloria had a sudden urge to tell her daughter her own story. The truth.

Everything about her marriage to her father. Tell her all about his philandering, his long travels, his risky business deals, her sleepless nights. How she was tricked into marrying him by her parents. Her pregnancies, births. To shake her and say, 'don't buy into it.'

To give her a choice to, perhaps, stay unmarried and devote her life to the opera. Gloria took another sip.

She held her emotions on reins with a skilful hand. Decades long training was highly efficient but took a lot of her energy. She rang the bell.

"'We'll get to it tomorrow."

Gerda was watching her mother and felt that something important just happened or was about to. That her experience, or rather lack of it let her mother down. She must ask her tomorrow. If only they'll be able to find time among all those guests coming here for the engagement party.

The valet came in with lemonade for Gerda. His mistress smiled," You are a treasure, Jan."

Gerda wanted to say 'Am I a nine year old?' but she didn't.

"You should change for dinner." It was again casual, as if there was nothing to talk about, no health, no future husbands, no opera. All was moving on the surface, lightly, speedily forward. In the center of life was the upcoming party. "Did your maid find the way to fix your dress?"

Gerda stood up. There was no trap, just the side door back into the house.

Only when she sat down on her bed did she allow herself to weep.

Her mother rang for her maid. "Marie, I will take a short stroll around the lake. Bring me my shawl."

Fountains were spurting water high toward the lucid blue of the skies. Wild ducks darted to the air from the glossy water. The evening was fragrant in the gardens around the castle. *Carl's castle!* Gloria shook her head and chuckled. She would have arranged things differently.

It was the last time Gerda saw her mother alive.

It was the Society Wedding of the Year __The most attractive heiress and the wealthy handsome chap. All newsreels shouted the headline to awestricken audiences all over the world.

Gerda was one of them _ Awestricken, and a bridesmaid, on top of it.

After her mother's funeral, time was so quiet. Too still. Too fragile to withstand. Unbearable. Mother's heart attack shocked them all. She went for a walk and never came back.

The original diagnosis was of a different kind, her end was exceptional luck. The verdict was a long debilitating disease. This lightning-like death was a blessing. They all tried to see it that way.

She was wrong about one thing. Her husband had known the whole time.

The doctor asked him to behave as he normally would have. Not to give his wife any reason to worry. He saw to it; his demands on her had never diminished. His impatience with her at times, his criticism of her housekeeping . . . He would walk out to the woods and cry.

Now, months later after the funeral, he needed some cheer. He suggested there be a wedding. No more waiting. A beautiful one; to honor his wife, to show the world!

Lieselotte von Bruck was marrying Gerda's favorite brother, Johann-Andreas .

Their father, dressed with his usual elegance in his morning suit, had a twig of white jasmine blossoms pinned to his gray lapel. He had planted a jasmine shrub in full bloom over his wife's grave in the garden. Her favorite scent. They said it would wither. It kept blooming! The most beautiful branch was in the large bouquet flowing down the bride's wedding dress. She wore the largest diamonds anyone had seen for a long time. He brought them from Africa.

The party was held in the bride's ancestral home. Tables bending under loads of delicacies, candle-lit regatta, fireworks with music, and everything you could fathom.

"Papa?" There, down by the lake, was a quiet oasis where the groom's father, Carl, found a little moment to himself.

"Gerda."

"Am I interrupting?"

"Oh no, darling . . . your mother and I just had a little talk."

Gerda smiled. She tried to follow suit and not be a sad, boring companion.

"She says you should get married." He was looking over the lake and reached for her hand without facing her. He felt her new heavy ring she inherited from Gloria.

"Does she, now?" Gerda whispered; the warmth of her father's palm had a reassuring effect.

"Anybody on your mind?"

No answer. A pause like that meant only one thing.

"Who is he?"

"What do you mean?"

"Child, child . . . I've known you since . . . before you were born, remember? So, who is he?" Gerda let go of his hand. She didn't plan this. She had no idea how to approach such a controversial announcement. "I wouldn't dare tell you his name, Papa."

"Why not? Is he a criminal?"

Gerda gave a start. "Why do you say that?"

"Now, is he?" Her father turned to face her.

"Of course not!" She was slightly offended but panicked; he saw that. It was a defense when she continued "I wouldn't have anything to do with such."

"Then tell me. Why is this so difficult?"

"You'll be cross."

"Try me." he was losing his patience. Gerda couldn't hesitate any longer.

"All right. I'll risk it. It's Marcel. Marcel Van Getz."

"Van Getz?"

Silence. Gerda was afraid to speak. He's mad at her. The pause was unbearable. It took him a moment before he organized his thoughts.

"Mother told me that you hated him. That he didn't behave like a gentleman."

"He didn't behave. . . ?" Gerda was puzzled. "He was always a perfect gentleman! I thought that it was you who didn't like him."

"No! I always admired his ways with money. Nice, clever chap, I thought."

Gerda couldn't believe this. All those years. . .

"Did he propose?" Her father side-glanced her.

"He doesn't know."

"What do you mean_he doesn't know?"

Silence. His little girl had no answer!

"Oh, my girl! If he's just a fantasy, do let it go. There are many more Marcels walking this Earth. Trust me."

"There's no one like him."

"Ah . . . so you have your mind firmly set, I see. There's danger in such force."

"I know, papa."

"Just don't get hurt."

"No," Gerda shook her head," I won't. Not now."

"You'll have my full support if you need it."

He pulled her to his side. There was his typical scent of expensive cigars and Eau de Cologne 4711, his choice for life. It had been too long since he planted a fatherly kiss in her hair. Waves and curls, just like when she was little; he wished she stayed clear from peroxide pale blond from a beauty salon in Vienna. *How much did that cost me?*

"Now, go my little girl. Let me tell the news to your mother." He caressed Gerda's hair, "And don't worry. I'll think of something clever so that she wouldn't be cross with us."

Helga was on the stage trying new versions of her speech after the rehearsal. She was very excited. Scared, but thrilled. She adored rehearsing. Rehearsing with Max in particular. No other theatre in the world was like his. There was a little voice in her head that would ask periodically: "Do you like rehearsing more than performing?" She didn't have a good answer to that impertinent question yet.

"You have a long-distance, Miss Dora!" Max Steinhardt's secretary peaked from the black velvet shawl of the left stage wing. Helga was sure the movie guy was calling back. She slipped into her heels and ran after Julia. "Coming!"

"Dora Glück speaking."

"Helga?"

"Bruno!"

There was a pause. Helga put down her book."Hullo! Bruno?"

"Helga, my dear!" there he was again. That must have been the long distance.

"What's happening in your realm? How's the new 'costume hanger', Adrianne?"

"She quit."

"What? Adrianne, quit? Oh, that's horrible!"

This call was much harder than he could have imagined. He had to tell her. It had to be him. Bruno couldn't make himself speak about it. He needed a little warm-up."Oh, it was . . . How's Berlin? Are you going to be a star soon? I need a guest star!"

"Not quite yet," Helga laughed. "But this has been the most exciting time of my life." She remembered who was on the other side of the line and quickly added. "Except for the time in your theatre, of course, darling."

She really meant it, didn't she? It sounded true and made him happy. She still belonged to his troupe. Bruno relaxed. They were friends. Forever. He took a deep breath and said in one note: "He's getting married."

"He? Who?"

Oh, the human heart! Bruno closed his eyes, bent his head. *She'd never even thought of that possibility, had she?* He shook his head. Gray hair bouncing on his temples in disbelieve, *She won't make this easy for me!* He opened his eyes and took a shot:

"Marcel . . . you know . . . he's getting married."

"Marcel? My Marcel?"

Oh, there it is . . . her Marcel . . . the girl just thinks that he would wait forever? Is it possible? An intelligent girl like Helga?

"I don't believe it."

"You'll be able to find it in any Society column soon."

The silence that followed was long. So long in fact, like the one onstage, when somebody forgets their line, humorously called the 'general pause.' Bruno didn't see any comeback in sight, nor any humor.

He wanted to say something nice, but relevant words escaped him. The silence was turning heavier by a second.

Helga hung up.

ACT VII

Gerda fastened her skirt, put on her blouse, and walked from behind the white screen.

The doctor finished his notes and took off his pince-nez. His fingers started gently massaging the root of his nose. There were two red marks. He wished he didn't need glasses yet, but his research. . . eyes glued to the microscope. "There's nothing wrong with you, Baroness."

Gerda sat down in the brown leather cushions of the round, mahogany armchair.

"But we've been trying for so long."

"It's been merely several months. All is normal. You have to relax."

"I did everything you suggested." Her head was making the mincing movements of disagreement. "I never stopped my sports; I try to keep our social schedule. I go skiing, boating, to the Riviera."

"Sometimes we see it as more of a psychological block . . . something from your childhood, from your past." The doctor stood up and walked around the oak desk to be closer to his patient.

"You are a catholic, Madame, if I am correct ?" He sat down on the corner of his desk.

"Isn't everybody in Austria?"

"Do you have a confessor?" continued the doctor, an atheist himself.

"Yes."

"Do you trust him with all of your thoughts, your inclinations?

"I do . . . implicitly . . ."

"Sometimes"—the doctor stood up again—"it can be a tiny detail, that you feel is of no importance, which could trigger some—he avoided exact words and rushed forward" It could help you get rid of some—doubts?" His time was precious. He sat back in his chair behind his vast desk. "A young, athletic woman like yourself will eventually get pregnant. I assure you." He seemed even more distant.

So did Gerda's face. Her elegant hand with a heavy diamond bracelet started pulling the fine, off-white, crocheted summer glove carefully over her many rings. "Thank you for your honesty."

"Not at all, Baroness. I will see you in three months."

"Yes . . . I suppose."

The doctor's secretary held the door for 'one of the most elegant women of Austria.' The headline in the magazine for ladies, which she reads under her desk in her spare time, was absolutely correct!

Some summer days were stuffy. But this thick, so early in the season? One crawled through the day without much to breathe . . . and her feet!

Bertha felt every cobblestone, every little pebble, through her worn-down heels. Her tired feet had been burning all day. You couldn't call these 'summer heels' but this was the pair she had stored away till the first true heatwave. Up till now, she walked around in her all-season heavy brown leather shoes.

She didn't realize how quickly she'd walked up to this church.

It was far from where she used to go. The enormity of the green cupola took her breath away.

Everything in her church was straight lines. Strict high gothic, it said on the placard by its door; tall, slender columns would lead your sight straight up to the heavens, without any rest for your eyes. The enormous stained-glass rosette over the church entrance brought colors on a sunny day into the otherwise dark, silvery space.

The church was cold. At first, when Bertha opened the small, heavy door into the wooden frame-and-glass enclosed vestibule, it was a nice change. Her cheeks were still hot from the outside. The wave of cold air greeted the young woman, as she crossed over the doorsill.

The echo of her hesitant steps announced the new visitor. The scent of incense invaded her nose, mixed further with the strong smell of beeswax from the myriads of dripping candles. Their straight flames were distracted only seldom by the door that opened and closed.

This church reminded her immediately of a lively afternoon in a Singspiel, the musical theater. The whole space was in the motion of gold, silver, crimson and blue. The diamond-studded stars of halos glittered above the heads of Saints. The nave was not dark; large windows, framed in meandering gilded frames, as if waves glistening in the rays of midday sunlight had arisen and splashed the frames with pure gold, filtered the outdoor light and allowed it to softly land within the sacred space. In this church, all movement was running upwards on a spiral. The whole space was as if floating in the air. Nothing seemed to be grounded. Bertha's eyes followed the swirling dramatic clouds escaping in the ceiling fresco up, up to the skies, to eternity, high above her head. Glistening gold, bright joyful colors, divinity, and angels all richly clad, all smiling as if having a party of sorts.

The wreath of side altars, on the outline of the church, was created with as much sublime inspiration as was the main altar in the middle of the misty space. The acute beauty of it all had struck Bertha down.

Marble of all colors was the material of the floor, altars, crosses. The eternal light by the tall altar was blinking unevenly through small red glass panes in the golden lamp. It was suspended from the high ceiling on long silver chains. To Bertha's eyes, it looked at least a hundred yards up. What a ceiling! It took Bertha's breath away. The tall cupola looked like a tunnel of clouds flying upwards to bright blue heavens. Bertha's head started spinning.

She could not explain what possessed her to enter. She stopped frequenting church after the Great War. Where was God that he could not visit the field in Oise where her brother had died in the deep mud of the battlefield?

The glitter and gloss of precious metals slipped out of focus and created a gleaming golden mist as Bertha's eyes filled up with tears. Bertha lifted her hand, dry, shriveled beyond its age, and brushed them to her side hair.

Her fingers, which used to be admired by her brother, pushed back one of her hairpins. In her thirty-fifth year, she was as tall as she was when she suddenly spurted up to her five feet at age of twelve. There and then she had stopped growing. Very early on she decided not to marry. She wanted to devote her life to her brother, help him grow his business. He was such a skillful carpenter!

Bertha's eyes welled up.

Why did I come here? She was walking slowly on the red sisal carpet from one of the gold and marble side-chapels to the other. Emotions had overwhelmed her. She was just passing a line of the wooden confessionals. Some of those "wooden booths" had their dark purple curtains open, some, where the priest was present, were closed as the confession is the most private matter.

Bertha's tears started running down her cheeks. She had no more strength to walk forward. Without thinking she sneaked into one of the confessionals and drew the curtain closed.

Bertha slouched down on the oak-wood bench, too big for her petite body. Her head bent down, ignoring the passage of time, she was weeping silently with all bitterness accumulated over the years. Bertha had not allowed herself to break down like this ever since that afternoon when the telegram about her brother's death was delivered from the War Office. She barely registered a new echo of steps coldly resonating in the high gilded space of this joyful baroque church. Another soul coming in for answers.

Bertha froze. She suddenly realized that she had sat down on the wrong side of the confessional. This was where the priest waits for someone's deepest secrets. She decided to step out. But her decision had come too late. The whole confessional shook from a heavy-boned body that just knelt down.

Bertha bent her head as low as the space allowed. She wished she could vanish. She tried not to breathe, not to listen.

The words of the sinner started coming in the expected order: the usual plea for forgiveness, which should have been followed by the actual sin. Bertha realized after a few moments, the same plea was coming over and over again. It seemed as if the sinner was unable to decide what to say. Then suddenly a muffled cry: "I murdered! God forgive me! I murdered."

The confessional shook again. Quick steps were vanishing in a frantic staccato towards the main door. Bertha was shocked. She stood up, confused; but her curiosity had grown stronger than her fear. She looked out.

There was the movement of light, well-made beige duster, its silhouette in the sun-backlit door frame; then the muffled sound of the heavy, tall carved doors closing in three separate motions. The church regained its quiet, passive beauty.

Bertha's quick steps almost ruined what was left of her heels.

On the top of the steep church staircase, out in full daylight, she had a good view over the entire street. Upon the hill, to her left, was a tall figure speeding up; Bertha saw the light duster, a fedora hat, now glossy in the sunlight, tilted deeply over the face.

Bertha started jogging. Right before the hill broke in half and ran down on the other side, she heard a car engine.

An elegant, visibly expensive, opened white sports car peeled off the curb. It started down the bright, wide avenue, its green leather interior shining in the sunlight. Bertha watched it as one would watch a cartoon movie: an object becomes smaller and smaller in the center of the screen until "The End" appears across the image, and ends an amusing afternoon.

Bertha didn't know what to do. She felt a tingling buzz in her forehead. The air was hot and she felt compelled to sit down on the church steps. She had a huge dilemma to solve.

On an impulse, she walked down the steps and crossed the street. Then, hesitantly, she walked up to a policeman standing on the corner of the main street.

He turned. Bertha gave a short, frightened sigh. No; he looked nothing like Herr Tonichek, from the street of her childhood; the fatherly friend who would wipe their noses and tuck in their shirts. Her confession had evaporated.

"Yes?!" His voice was as sharp as his look. He was hot and thirsty.

"I-I am sorry, I think I got . . . lost"—Bertha spat out her lie—"tramway number thirteen?"

"Can't you see?" He pointed across the square. "Right over there!"

Bertha turned and was in a hurry to turn the corner.

The policeman looked in confusion as she started in the opposite direction. "Some people got the nerve!" He tossed after her. She couldn't care less.

Bertha absentmindedly stepped into a small cinema. She needed to think. It was a small bio, the biograph, that played all day long. You could enter and for the price of one ticket stay all day.

They were showing the Greta Garbo movie she'd seen already twice. Perfect for thinking. She sat down on the hard wooden seat. She kept sitting upright as if she was wearing a corset. The lights were brought up a little. The small space was half empty. The day was too beautiful to come here. Loved-up couples, and some Garbo fans. People were coming and leaving, some rushing to the loo and back, the black satin-white apron clad woman was selling the ice called 'Eskimo.' Arms in the air to get her close, her loud counting and 'Your change. Here is your Eskimo, sir' made Bertha's head pounding.

She wasn't paying much attention to the weekly newsreel up on the screen. Cars!

Male toys had no charm without her brother next to her. Her eyes welled up again.

She blinked and started looking for her handkerchief. A high, nasal-sounding voice was announcing enthusiastically. "The brand new . . . with bespoke green leather seats . . . priced for." The quoted value was so astronomic that Bertha's shocked brain woke up. She looked up at the screen. The cameraman moved closer. Bertha's eyes froze on the image. She didn't know cars, but she recognized this one.

The high voice kept gushing, "There is only one person, in all of Austria, driving this very new white Bugatti at the moment." Bertha forgot to breathe. She got the name.

She moved her feet back in her old patent shoes. How many layers of polish before they disintegrate? She spat out loud, "There is no God."

An angry "shh!" catapulted her from her seat.

Back on the busy afternoon street, Bertha's small fist clenched tightly her hand-down brown purse. Her headache was gone. For the first time in many years, she gave an audible laugh.

"Baron Van Getz!"

"Gerda?" Marcel looked up from his morning newspaper. "Gerda?" His wife was holding a tall crystal glass full of orange juice. She forgot to drink. "What?"

"Are you alright?"

"Yes, perfect. I am just thinking." She took a gulp. "We could move somewhere else . . . somewhere by the seaside . . . maybe . . .?"

"Is that what your doctor says?"

"My doctor? Why my doctor?"

"Because I just received his bill, darling, and it occurs to me, that not everything is, perhaps, all right, as you keep telling me."

He placed his unlit cigarette on the green, barge-on-waves piece of pottery ashtray.

"Come on, girl. What can I do?"

"Let's move away. Let's travel the world. Let's . . . move to America!"

"Gerda?" Marcel was laughing. "What got into you, girl?"

She cuddled up close to him. "I am bored. That's what. When I'm bored you will soon be bored with me, and I fear that moment."

"Nonsense! You are not going to bore me. Ever. That's as simple as that."

"Think about what fun we could have traveling together."

"Stop right there. You know how often I have to travel." He stood up and left her in the cold of the room without any support. "No more aircraft." Marcel lit his cigarette. "No more ocean liners." He exhaled habitually in puffs. The cigarette smoke created rings that floated across the middle of the room.

For the first time ever, Gerda didn't feel like running and poking them with her fingertips. Her fingers felt suddenly too heavy; her hands too big. His decisions were final. She learned that the hard way. He was very much like her father. She's never seen it so clearly before.

When Marcel left for his work Gerda opened the bottom drawer in her white and chrome dressing-room. There, folded into four, was the letter that came last night. The envelope was addressed to "Van Getz". The handwriting was odd. For no reason, its untidiness alarmed her. Against her habit she took it. Against common sense, she read it after Marcel fell asleep.

"I know you murdered." was the brief opening sentence. Gerda's night lost its comfort.

"I heard you in the church."

After that, it stated the place, time, and the demanded sum of money. Gerda had to sit down.

Who is this blackmailer? What does he know?

She walked to her pristine bathroom and drank streams of ice-cold water straight from the gilded tap. It ran to her ears and in her hair; she didn't even notice. Dripping everywhere as she walked across the parqueted floor, she returned to reread the blackmail. It was only now, once she calmed down a little, that she noticed the writing paper_ it was a rectangular cut-out from a paper flour-bag. Gerda's sense of her own power returned. She saw the social distance between her fine, bespoke writing paper; perfumed and with a golden line running all around. Her coat-of-arms, embossed in gold, shone in the letterhead. That's where her duty lies. She is Van Getz now. Gerda took a deep breath and as if in front of the full theatre house, said: "Baroness Marcel Van Getz."

Bertha turned, her face was blank. Heart in her throat took on the quick time of her feet. They carried her away as if she became a figure of the mechanical Bethlehem in her church at Christmas. She walked as if in a daydream. Not really present but aware. Her old heels painfully wiggled over the unearthed pebble stones of the rain-washed country road. Her temples were still pounding. She pressed her chin down. It got caught in the sour smell of her body. It couldn't stop her now. Her odor was barely covered by the cheapest of soaps.

Under her breath, she whispered "Nothing less than French perfumes!"

Yes. That's what she's going to buy first! The most expensive French perfume. *That's what I'm going to wear from now on!* She was promising herself with every uneven step that she would never smell of anything but luxury.

Now she knew that her heart would always stay calm through all of the next times she's going to come here, over and over again. Bertha smiled. Her brother had always complimented her lovely smile. She's going to buy herself an expensive lipstick . . . and a white-bristle toothbrush!

She started walking away alongside the riverbank. The weather was warm, the air scented with the sweet honey of blooming linden trees. The perfume of summer was catching in Bertha's hair. She couldn't stop smiling; she felt the weight of her purse, now filled up with large banknotes.

"It went better than I thought!" It made her gloriously proud and happy without any tint of guilt; "I've got money!" Her face kept grinning not just because of the bright sun. A new world opened in front of her "I deserve it . . . all of it!" She lifted her bulging purse up and pressed it on her chest.

The powerful hit of steel from behind broke Bertha's body instantly. The white car backed up and finished the murder.

A heavy-boned body slipped out of the fine green leather seat. Gerda bent down. Her mind was working precisely like her golden Swiss wristwatch. Her slim hands enveloped tightly in elegant, fashionable gloves, took out all of the banknotes from Bertha's handed-down brown purse. Gerda glanced around. The place was as deserted as she'd always remembered it from her rendezvous. She tossed the purse into the river.

Bertha's body was not heavy for an athlete like Gerda. It was a short walk down to the stream.

The water closed darkly above Bertha's first, and last attempt at blackmail.

The river was running away, carrying all secrets dutifully within its body of water, far, forward, towards the unknown.

The field-road dust, warm on a hot day like this, was slowly settling back down in the layers of light grays and yellows; in a translucent choreography behind the leaving car, one cloud of microscopic particles after another was slowly descending with the occasional improvised twirl of a dust devil.

Then there was only the sound of buzzing bees, the cool glissando of the river current, the warm scent of flowers growing wildly underneath the ancient trees. The white Bugatti was far away on the horizon. Its image was getting smaller and smaller. Just like in the movies, right before the moment when the last words The End appear across the screen to announce another full-stop after an amusing afternoon.

Gerda had to control her foot on the accelerator. She wanted to be away from the river as far as possible. Her heart pounding, her eyesight compromised, she was stirring her car as if blindfolded. She started feeling faint, then cramps overpowered the lower part of her body. She didn't want to stop. Whatever this was she will overcome it.

She has to breathe. *It's just nerves. All will be well soon.* Her foot added speed. She zoomed through a small town not looking at the mortified group of people who jumped back off the road at the last second. She saw church steeples, cupolas, and the Prater wheel. She slowed down a bit as she approached the town. Then there came a long curve . . .

When Gerda woke up Marcel was standing above her. She wanted to tell him that she had to protect them. He was calm, his face washed with . . . tears?

"What happened?"

"That's all right, darling. It will happen again. They are certain now."

"What will happen again . . . ?" Gerda's mind was confused from the anesthetic.

"We should leave," said the doctor. "She lost a lot of blood."

"Did I hurt someone?"

"No, not you, my darling. Don't think. Sleep."

She tried to smile at Marcel but all went dark again and she floated back to a dreamless sleep.

Marcel was sitting in his vast office. He didn't have to look around. He was smoking, looking out the window, and feeling his room. As if it was the presence of a good friend to whom you don't have to explain anything. He adores Art Deco. He surrounded himself with everything he could to fill in their new house, his office, their country retreat.

So, she was pregnant after all . . . What will happen now? The doctors couldn't say.

They suggested it could be just the beginning of many to come . . . and of course this could be it, forever.

He was honest enough to admit to himself that he was not exactly in deep passionate love with Gerda. But he truly liked her. His young wife: athletic, quick, charming, and a consummate trickster!

He smiled. She changed her appearance to trick him! *Touché!* It kept amusing him. He'll never forget how he met the 'unknown' young woman when he first met her in Vienna.

It was his close friend at the time, Monique, who brought her to a party in his new house after Helga left.

"Marcel, I want you to meet my new friend." The name was a blur, of no importance to him at that point. The young woman stepped forward.

She was a stunning tall redhead with a pleasant smile. She was superbly dressed. That made an impression on a snob like Marcel.

He could have sworn he knew her well. Probably from a magazine cover? He didn't hesitate to ask.

Oh no. She'd just arrived from Paris. Her family wouldn't appreciate her modeling or any kind of demi-monde associations.

Which was just as well. With Helga gone, after Adrianne left Vienna, Marcel lost his appetite for operetta. Plus, there were rumors around that theatre that could have put his reputation in jeopardy. He was smart not to return.

"Alone in Vienna?"

She nodded, her bright green chrysoprase and diamond earrings swayed. Marcel looked at her slender hand. Those were not pieces of costume jewelry. There was a fine feeling of familiarity around her. He couldn't stop talking, trying to amuse her, trying to . . . well, seduce her . . . he's Marcel.

He put all aces in front of her: He has the Opera abonnement, (He chose not to mention he hated opera) then there will be a party to celebrate his birthday next week; then there's an opening of the Art Gallery in . . .

She said 'Yes' to all of them.

Her eye-catching dress, the low-cut brilliantly embroidered number was no doubt the new model from Poiret-Paris. He recognized it. He wanted to invest with them.

She took a careful sip from her cocktail. The two oval, bright green chrysoprase beads on each end of the long lariat had a tendency to hide inside the low-cut back neckline. His fingers longed to follow them there.

"What's your name?"

"Why don't you choose one for me?" She was full of surprises. He blundered spontaneously: "Gerda." He surprised himself. *Why did I say that?* There must have been something about her. A small detail that was stored in the back of his memory.

She laughed with such joy: "Very well, then, Gerda it is!"

Marcel was amused. Had no clue. She didn't allow him to drive her home but ordered a taxi. He was interested. She cautiously trod forward. Marcel's experienced eyes saw it, and he opened the door.

Gerda's sleep was anesthetic-induced; sickening, surreal at times. She was recalling parts of the puzzle she'd been living the last year. She couldn't fit the pieces properly together.

A bright-green box of a telephone attached to a long line was handed to her. The most familiar voice sounded tired but excited. "Any progress?"

"Papa!" Gerda laughed and undid her earring. "Where are you?" She took the other off as well and handed them to her maid. She was the chorus girl in the Treasures of Asia. . .

"I'm across the street in a telephone booth."

"Wait, there's no telephone b—"

"Of course not!" He was laughing out loud.

"Oh, Papa! You got me there." She heard in his voice where she got her impatience and curiosity from. She had a glittering wand in her hand. There was Helga ready to step on stage. To push her from the stage, to poke her eyes!

"Tell me everything . . . and I mean everything."

"Help me." She couldn't remember what it was she wanted to tell him. "Papa. I think . . . I. . . I . . ." Her body felt so light again. There was white cotton all around her. It was pushing to her eyes, she felt it in her mouth. "I think I murdered someone."

Marcel lit another cigarette and poured himself another glass of whisky. He didn't bother with ice. His mind was playing a curious, exciting, puzzling movie in his mind. He was surely never bored with Gerda. Oh, the night she decided to 'place-her-cards-on-the-table!'

That restaurant was the best in Vienna. In Marcel's opinion, this restaurant had it all: music and hyper-modern decor. Good cuisine, but the draw was the dancing floor here. Amusing entertainment, good wine.

It made him smile still. He never asked her real name. He wasn't over Helga in fact; this was a girl for "in-between." At that time they'd been seeing each other for almost a month, most days. Some evenings, too, but it was as platonic as he could stand it. That was new to him. Marcel felt that he wouldn't be able to continue this restraint game for much longer.

The orchestra started playing quiet background music when she chose to enter.

Marcel spotted her bright orange and grey glittering dress like everyone else here. She was "Stunning!" Her tall figure looked familiar to all. She looked like a model, like. . . a famous actress.

The short train was flickering behind her ankles as she walked towards Marcel. Her hair was under a tight black turban glistening with intricate orange beadwork; long diamond and red coral earrings were swinging in the rhythm of her gait. There was a brief moment when Marcel could have sworn he knew her once. The way she held her face. The way she animated her body. . .

She was not alone. She was coming on the arm of an older gentleman. Smiling broadly, she said without any apology; "Marcel, you know my father."

Marcel's hand stayed suspended in the passage between him and his former "little" Gerda's parent, the successful banker, Carl Sommer. Then he turned to Gerda. "Gerda?" He was caught by surprise, amused, feeling unexplainable joy, all at once. He glanced at this charming young tall woman. Not a hint of the little girl with cherries hung around her petite ears. *She's like no one I have ever met.* Marcel produced a cliché while stretching his arm to shake hands with her father. "Why didn't you tell me...?"

The trio turned all heads at that place!

Carl Sommer was as jovial as Marcel used to know him before . . . well, a long time ago. "What a pleasant evening to be with our old friend."

"Gerda! You little mischief! I was sure I knew you from somewhere."

She didn't feel like explaining anything. This evening was going as planned.

"Here, I wanted to give this back to you." Gerda took a small glistening object from her small, triangular diamanté reticule.

The maître d' came to take their orders. When he left Marcel looked at the small box Gerda pressed into his palm. "My vesta? But it was a present from me."

"Not this one." This was not the place to tell him the whole truth yet. She made a funny 'guilty' face and whispered loudly, "I pinched this one from your pocket." She couldn't help to send a provocative look at her father. Her lips pursed, her upper body quickly swayed. She took a sip from her cocktail.

It was well calculated. He was shocked. "You did what?" Or was he, indeed? She bit in the olive and twirled the short metal skewer.

Little girl Gerda! Marcel was more amused than ever. She surely looks exquisite, she's not dumb, she's undeniably sexy, she's got a sense of humor. There will never be a lack of money . . . Perhaps she is the right wife for him.

Marcel proposed that week.

Gerda woke up. Her nose was overpowered by the hospital disinfectants. Iodine, vinegar . . . She couldn't recall what happened.

Then suddenly everything came into focus. The woman _ her blackmailer. The way her face was victorious, self-assured, proud!

Gerda started sobbing. The nurse rushed to her room. "Madame Van Getz, here, this will help." She placed a pill on Gerda's tongue. It was bitter. Before she could spit it out cold water inundated her mouth. Gerda started swallowing. The nurse wiped her mouth. Gerda looked at her with suspicion, "Why am I here?"

"You don't remember?"

"No. I don't know . . . how I got here?"

"You had an accident . . . a car accident."

"My car?"

"Yes. Your car."

"Did anybody get hurt?!" The panic was genuine.

"You did, Madame. Badly."

"My face?"

"No, no . . . not your face."

Gerda moved her arms. They were fine too. She carefully refocused on her legs. All there and working . . . what a relief! "What's wrong then?"

"You lost . . ." The nurse regretted immediately saying that. She was not supposed to give her the tragic news.

"What did I lose?" Gerda raised her voice.

Her doctor entered and the nurse was suddenly busy elsewhere.

Gerda needed her answer, she started being hysterical "Doctor . . . what did she mean?"

He took her wrist in his cool fingers; his arm moved up and back to free his wristwatch from under his sleeve. She hated him for his slow ways! He took her pulse, touched her forehead, and placed the black rubber ends of his stethoscope in his ears. The nurse was back to open the front of her sleeping gown. Without care, he put the cold, round metal on her chest. Gerda's body gave a startle.

"Try not to move, please. Give me a deep breath." He listened carefully to her heart, her lungs. Then his hands folded his tool and instead of hanging it around his neck, he stuffed it in the pocket of his white frock. "I'm sorry, Baronesse, I didn't catch your question."

Gerda was certain that he was lying. She had to know the truth. "Your nurse said: 'you lost it.' What did I lose?" the moment she said it out loud it was clear to her.

Her sobs washed away all previous sorrows this room had seen before. Her desperation was of a different kind. "I was . . . I was . . . I . . . I lost my baby?"

"Nurse, here, quickly!"

The shot worked almost immediately. Her doctor stayed until she started breathing evenly. He was certain that she was hallucinating when she whispered to him, her eyes closed, "I had to . . . and now . . . life for life."

But he didn't mention it to her husband, or to anybody.

ACT VIII

———⚬⚬⚬❦⚬⚬⚬———

The 1930s

"**M**iss Dora?" Helga was looking out the window towards the grandiose trees in the park on the horizon. She gave Max Steinhardt's secretary a blank look. "Mr. Steinhardt will see you now."

Helga stepped inside the legendary office which he designed.

"Come in and sit." This was not his usual imperative tone; here was that rumor about his new venture across the Ocean. He didn't seem to find time to tell her. Her only interpretation was that she was not included. In her mind, she was packing for her way back to Vienna.

Helga didn't sit. He added one more brief, swift movement of his fountain pen on the top paper and closed the folder he was working on. It briefly interrupted the silence charged with anticipation. "Do sit down."

Helga saw a strange gentleman with him last week. An American, she was told. A film producer. She sat down and remained on the edge of the black leather upholstered chair.

"I received an offer to do a movie."

His secretary came in; he handed her the folder. "I signed only the second one . . . The first proposal I'm still not sure about. Call them."

"Certainly, sir."

He turned to Helga. "You were not in my production of that Shakespeare; I think that you—"

Helga moved to the very edge of the chair ready to stand up.

"Laura!" He called after his secretary, "Tell them I'll telephone tomorrow." Then he turned back to Helga. "I'm convinced that you should come with us to America, to do the screen tests for Titania."

Helga stood up; her face like a freshly washed window pane.

He walked to the heavy, black bookshelves taking the full wall of his green-carpeted office. Helga sat back. Max walked to her and placed a volume of bound papers in Helga's lap. "Learn the part, as is, in this book. These are my rewrites."

"Oh. Of course, yes, I will."

"I'm going to direct the screen tests because I will direct the movie."

"Of course, you will." Helga was astounded. In her mind, she unpacked for Vienna and started making lists of things to take to America.

Max went to the window and opened it. He took one deep breath and shut the window.

"Brr . . . too cold."

For the first time since she entered today, he looked at her. "Come here, my girl. It's been months too long. You haven't had any time for me lately."

"I haven't?" She smiled at him. "Max, are you sure you have time for this?"

"Yes. I'm sure. I will always have time for this. I want this. I'll see you tonight."

"If you say so . . . I'll be waiting." Helga received his kiss as a seal on their brief meeting.

Her impatient self was already on the ocean liner. That's when she'll finally have 'time for this'. She looked at the fascicle of Max's re-writes. It just occurred to her that she memorized Shakespeare's text. The pleasure turned to a nightmare written in Max's ink. Helga couldn't think of anything as hard as trying to override one Genius with the other.

Marcel was taking out his cufflinks. "That was a long opera."

Gerda laughed from her exquisite crystal mirror. "It's your music education…"

"Only for you!" Marcel blew her a kiss. She was taking her diamond earrings off. She put them carefully in the small, cube-like green velvet box.". . . Carmen. What could be better?" Her maid took it and turned to leave.

"Wait, here!" Gerda walked up to her and hung the black pearl and diamond sautoir around the maid's neck "So that you don't have to come back again."

"Thank you, madame." She turned at the door and curtseyed. "Good night, madame. Good night, my lord."

"You are always so thoughtful," commented Marcel from his wardrobe corner once the maid left. "Carmen. . . too emotional. Dark passions. Not my thing."

Gerda was spreading cold cream all over her face. She didn't want to ask him 'what thing' was his. He watched her ritual, fascinated: small circles in between her eyebrows, larger on her cheekbones, tiny taps under her eyes. She looked at him "Upbringing . . . I assume." He wasn't sure if that was a delayed answer. Her chestnut hair was held back with a soft, white headband.

Marcel walked out from his mahogany, cedarwood inlaid dressing room. He stopped behind her tabouret, then said casually:

"Whatever happened to that other silver vesta of mine. . . I've been wondering. . ." He looked through the modern, angular mirror at her white face, ". . . my dear clown?" He bent down and kissed her nape. "New perfume?"

The tone was calming, allowing her to say casually "Oh . . . that vesta!" And she changed the subject " . . . this is my usual Number One . . . I haven't worn anything else since."

"Yes, the silver one I gave you as a gift when you were a little girl."

The strategic maneuver seemed not to be working. Gerda's creative mind started looking for a new one "Oh, I don't know . . . I think my mother must have taken it from under my pillow."

Marcel walked away from her and sat down on their bed. "From under your pillow?" Then, balancing on the tightrope of melancholy he winked at her," Wipe your white face, my dear clown; and come here . . . you romantic." Gerda looked at herself in the mirror __ *It worked!*

The elevator stopped. Gerda pushed the inner folding door to the side and opened the outer one. It was made of flat black metal bars. Simple, cage-like. A metaphor. Perhaps. Was she right to come here? Was it reasonable? She hesitated. There was really nothing she could put her finger on. Just Marcel the way he's always been around women. Since Helga's vanishing, she hasn't had reason to worry.

It was the third floor, as the business card in her hand indicated. Gerda stepped out of the elevator.

The bell made a screeching sound, like a sports car driving too fast, cutting the curve of the road without slowing down. She rang one more time. Her impatience building up, Gerda reached for the brass gadget again when the door opened.

A young man, not more than thirty, perhaps thirty-five. *Men keep their looks. How unfair.* He was almost as tall as she was, said with a slight bow of his dark blond head, "We've been expecting you, Baroness."

She followed him through a narrow, dark hallway. No carpet. Her heels were announcing her arrival. The hallway turned at a right angle to the left.

An unexpectedly bright, square living room was furnished with good taste, inviting.

It was a corner apartment with large modern windows. "Meet my associate, Robert Weiss." Another young man, tall, athletic, blond curls falling on his forehead, rose from his chair; it was a natural part of his 'Hello.' His eyes were trying not to fall over the new client's looks. That small gesture made her feel immediately better. His enthusiasm flattered.

"Please, sit down."

Yes, she will stay. She didn't shake hands with either of them, merely acknowledged their greetings with a light smile. The armchair was modern. No luxury, but good. She slipped in and crossed her legs at ankles. The curl still over his forehead, the young associate sat back. Gerda had an acute urge to brush it off his forehead.

"What can we do for you, Baroness?" The young man, who met her at the door, sat down behind a massive, modern desk of almost orange knot-oak; covered in high-gloss veneer it was reflecting the bright room with all of its objects.

"I need you to follow my husband."

His associate took a black box with mother-of-pearl geometric inlays from the glass top of the coffee table. "Would you care for a cigarette, Baroness?"

Gerda's hand gesture was elegantly executed No. Her dark-blue straw hat with a narrow brim moved ever so slightly. "No, thank you." Her veil was cutting on the slant across her features.

"What can you tell me about . . .?" The pleasant voice came across the large desk.

"There's not much that you wouldn't find in any social-gossip column. Mister. . ." She fished for the business card she had absentmindedly put in her purse, ". . . Mister. . ."

"Jacob Holzknecht, at your service."

Gerda smiled as an obligation. Jacob was certain that he must have seen her face somewhere before. Her head moved to the profile. No, he couldn't swear he had. She crossed her legs in her long skirt one more time. Something about her . . . He will remember eventually. So, this is the new Baroness Van Getz? Marcel wasn't that crazy about Helga after all. Shame. Jacob liked Helga. Her kindness to Zelli. That flashback hurt. What does Marcel see in this girl? He couldn't imagine Helga coming for help here.

"Are we waiting for someone else?" Gerda hasn't time for lingering.

Jacob Holzknecht, the private investigator, executed one of his polite smiles, and asked with professional interest "Would you mind to elaborate, Baroness ?"

The voyage across the Atlantic was a grueling one. How much easier was the train ride from California to New York! But that was part of Helga's decision. She wasn't inclined to stay in Hollywood.

The last months had changed Max; he wasn't as she'd adored him before anymore. 'And no, his decision to give the role of Titania to that American actress had nothing to do with it . . .' She could already hear herself answering a cinema magazine reporter.

Helga looked above her. Broken lines of sunlit waves were reflecting on the bright white overhang of the cabins. She had such a blast while it all lasted . . . such a line of amazing work . . . no, not work_ it was all like a dream; all of her fantasies about what theatre could be like, realized. Ever since she read about Max as a young woman, back at school, in Switzerland . . .

Helga reached behind her head, pulled down the woolen blanket that was folded there; she covered her shoulders with the grey and red plaid and crossed it over her breasts. Max Steinhardt . . . that was such a dream; all of that was suddenly hers, until . . . until it was not. One blanket wasn't enough; the breeze from the sea waves was cold. She reached for the identical one on the chair backrest next to her.

Perhaps, it didn't get colder tonight. She looked across the deck. The chill was her nerves.

She knew it was. An unending mass of water in front of her . . . no land on the horizon. What a splendid metaphor for her days in Berlin at Max Steinhardt's Theatre.

Max Steinhardt changed her life; he's done it so many times for so many artists . . . it was a never-ending feast of exciting meetings, gatherings, talks into wee hours . . . plans, plans, and more plans . . . projects of Gargantuesque proportions, plays for intimate spaces, robust Greek dramas for thousands of spectators, film, design . . . legendary names, men, women. Helga never ceased to be surprised. It was an unresting flow of, "Dora, this is . . . Dora, meet my friend . . . I want you to meet." It was wonderful.

As the reputation he'd built up over the years grew, his fame became universal, his many theatres became major centers for everything new, and experimental; everybody was equal there: actors, designers, composers; he was the ever-present Hand of Gods, Larger than Life, and more inventive than any man in theatre she'd ever heard of.

And yes . . . she must admit to herself; she's been hurt. She was absolutely certain that the part of Titania in his film was for her. The people around him made her think that . . . all of those "good friends" who meant "only the best for you, d'ah'lin'." Show business . . .

Helga's black painted eyelash got stuck on the other. Her index finger brushed them to fix that; habits. Even here she wore full makeup, she dressed up with care. An ocean liner is an incubator of opportunities. Especially here, in the first class.

The deck started slowly filling up with people taking a stroll before dinner.

She was good at putting herself in a good mood. Sometimes it took a while but never failed. Happiness is a choice, she read somewhere. Her face warmed up with a smile. She will stop first in London, then in Paris; to shop for the new season. She didn't mean the theatre season. Then she would go back to Berlin, pack her things and move back to . . . Vienna? Perhaps . . . maybe to a different type of theatre . . . a cabaret for a change? Steinhardt's theatre without the orchestra in the pit, the intimacy of a smaller space, the immediacy of reaction. Speaking her lines practically to her spectator's faces. She wants more of that now. Her friend Sybille said something about the opening of small theatre space . . . She had some ideas of that sort. Her and her husband . . . but it was before . . . "Before I got murdered." Even in such a light whisper, it shocked her again. Unexpectedly. Deeply.

That horrific day stayed in her mind like a movie reel; as a soundstage which she had accidentally entered, and exited before anyone noticed.

She read in the news that Marcel's company had moved to Switzerland. Was it Geneva? She saved his life. She prevented his ruin. *His being hanged for Zelda's murder!*

A horrid thought . . . to lose him! What was the chance to trip on his silver vesta as she did? What luck!

There were times when she wanted to go back to Vienna and tell him. Make it clear that she forgave him. That she had never stopped longing for him. Despite what happened down in the Maze. Because of it.

Helga took a look over the darkening body of water. She tried to look over the calm waters as far as she could see. He will never know.

"Would you mind if I smoke here?" a stranger stopped in the hope for a conversation.

"Not at all."

"May I offer you . . . ?"

"Yes . . . yes, you may."

The stranger stepped closer; his cigarette case opened in his hand.

Helga's face lit up. The voyage just changed its character.

His upper body bent "Have we met before?"

This would have been a cliche of cliches but because of her public persona he gave it a chance. "Perhaps. Try."

"I would have sworn I'd seen you somewhere in. . ." he tried to place her. "In a theatre?" was his careful guess.

Helga was amused. "Have you?"

"Movies?"

"Helas."

"Which city?"

"Vienna, maybe. Berlin, a possibility."

"Definitely not Berlin."

The sky made one last big splash of sunlight. Helga's face brightened in the soft yellow gleam. The young man tossed his head back in a burst of laughter. "Helga Hayden! I saw you in *Rosenkavalier* when I was a student."

That last remark wasn't necessary! thought Helga with slight irritation. Is she getting old?

Her initial enthusiasm for the prospect of this voyage has been turned to 'a man overboard'.

Calm down. There are many days ahead. Solitude is not your strongest suit. Helga Hayden, the Viennese operetta star, commanded herself and returned effortlessly to the year before her Berlin engagement:

She picked a cigarette from his silver, blue-enameled cigarette case. Slow roll in her fingers. The smell of figs. The first whiff of fragrant tobacco. Her smile was like a smooth cocktail when she asked "What were you up to in America, Mr. . . ?"

"Doctor Böhm, from Vienna. Just in New York for a week. A conference of physicians."

"A doctor?"

"A spine specialist. How's your back?"

Did he wink at her? Helga giggled. *Perhaps I am not getting old just yet.* "It might need some attention, perhaps."

Helga savored her cigarette, "How are the spines of my competition in Vienna these days?" Helga exhaled away from his face.

"Some are pretty spineless. Brownshirt seemed to be the scream of the season." His news was nothing to burst out laughing about. Just a sad chuckle and they kept smoking.

His humor was balancing on the edge of darkness. It pleased her. He observed the same in her. "I am afraid that times are getting more complicated . . ."

Helga's blankets started falling; he tilted his head, his cigarette pushed to his mouth's corner, "Allow me." The loud brass ship-bell announced dinner. He helped her to stand up, "Some people don't seem to notice that change."

"Perhaps, after dinner, we could come back here?" Helga took off the blankets; he helped her put them aside. Her ankle-length golden lamé dress caught the light from the setting sun. The back neckline was low.

"Maybe not here." He took off his jacket and arranged it around her shoulders. "It's getting cold."

"Yes, doctor!" Helga smiled and felt a new wave of joy from their meeting.

What luck I decided against flying.

He offered her his arm; she took it with ease. He felt her body warming up his thin fine-cotton shirt. From the distance, they looked like a married couple still enviably happy beyond the seven years' proverbial mark.

Gerda stretched her suntanned arm across the small round tabletop. The white marble was cold but she didn't notice.

Golden bracelets slid over her wrists with several hollow clicks. They were very much out of their class there. She took the large brown envelope from Jacob Holzknecht's hands a second before he offered it. Her spectacular diamond ring sent a quick sequence of crisscrossing bolts of lightning towards the small bistro ceiling.

"There's nothing to report so far, Baroness." Gerda inserted her index finger under the fold and pushed it up. She tilted it and widened the view with two fingers. She peaked at the top photo. "Hm. It was probably just my imagination . . . "Gerda lifted her arm, golden bracelets traveled in the opposite direction with more noise "Waiter!"

Jacob was hesitant. "It's been months and . . . I don't want to waste your money."

She returned the envelope to him. "It's my money. My money is of no concern of yours." She sat up straight, abruptly. Her impatient tone changed to irritated, "I'll do with it as I choose."

"Yes, of course, madame, I apologize." She saw this young man, not much older than her, trying to make his living. She leaned back on the Thonet chair.

"No harm done." The waiter arrived.

"Irish coffee, and"—she looked back at Jacob—"what will you have?"

Jacob's pause made her say, "You are invited."

He blushed. "Turkish then. Thank you."

Cute, she thought.

"Stay the course after my husband returns from South America." She felt a sudden urge to explain. "You see . . . I don't even know why I hired you. There has never been anybody else for my husband except me. Do you understand? Ever. Since I was a young girl. My husband is not that sort of man." Their coffees arrived. She sipped hers right away. It almost scalded her tongue. She needed activity now. Moving forward. Waiting until Jacob's sugared coffee was transferred from 'dzezva' to his small cup was beyond her patience.

"Yes, of course, Baroness."

"I've known him since my childhood . . . he never turned into a womanizer like some men."

"Yes, I understand." Jacob was glad he could take a sip of his thick, sweet treat.

"Do you? He's the most wonderful husband. . . the most caring . . ." Gerda was looking for more superlatives. "The perfect one," she concluded in, what looked like, a proclamation of victory. Jacob couldn't wait to be out of there.

Jacob Holzknecht pulled over the first chance he had. With the engine off, he remained sitting. He stayed in his old car, motionless, his thoughts running in high gear. Now he was faced with an unexpected dilemma: should or should not he tell his client, this obviously naive, nice young woman the truth? Was it possible to tell the young Baronesse van Getz, that he knew her husband years ago; that Marcel is everything but; that somewhere in the world there's still that one woman Marcel would run back to? Or, should he pretend he'd never met him?

Jacob touched his wallet. It was a worn-down blue leather Zelda had bought him for Christmas. He took out one photo he had been carrying around all these years.

It was a small snapshot he took on the beach: Zelda in her swimsuit, her French-terry bathing robe's hood down, balancing on one bent leg, the other in the air pressed next to her naked knee, open Chinese sun-umbrella over her shoulder like a halo. It was a palm-sized rectangle with white edges, trimmed with wavy sheers. It sums her up perfectly.

He tried to think what Zelda would have advised him to do. His clever girl. His troubled girl. Finished off by a drug dealer. Shot in her back. He'll find that beast one day. He swore it.

Jacob's love for the woman he adored like no other had never diminished. A loss so tragic, that had left him speechless for years; so powerful that he couldn't feel, couldn't think for the first long months afterward. He started working again only to find her murderer; he promised he would accomplish it in his lifetime, no matter what it takes. For that he needed money. There was his answer.

He put the snapshot carefully back in his wallet and cranked up his old, black Stayer.

"Taxi!" Helga was late. She hated being late. Only that the shopping was too much fun. She promised to be at her hotel, by her phone, by three; her friend Sybill's call will be coming for her from Vienna. Now, this. "C'mon!" No taxi in sight. It was raining. *London. Typical.*

She walked up the road towards the Embassy mile. *No taxi?* It came to her suddenly. This is Mayfair, of course! Everybody has a chauffeur here. Surprise! As if to question her argument, a taxi appeared from around the corner. Helga lifted her arm "Taxi!" she shouted on top of her lungs. The moment the driver opened the door, she pushed around the leaving passenger to get out of the rain.

"Helga!"

Helga froze. She wasn't sure if she actually heard her name . . . afterward she was never sure if she said his name. But she stopped; frightened the second he turned and stepped back in the taxi with her. 'Frightened' was exchanged for 'blissfully happy.' Marcel touched her hair.

"What a brilliant change." He didn't remove his eyes from her eyes. Like on their very first meeting they were already part of each other's existence.

"I wouldn't have recognized you from a distance."

The cab driver was confused when he asked. "Where to?"

"Wait here!" answered Marcel with his usual authority; then to Helga, with all of his tenderness "I'll be only a minute! I promise, darling" and off he went inside the embassy.

Helga had a chance to tell the driver to take off, but she couldn't.

There, right there, she stopped running away from Marcel. All she wanted at this minute was him. It was madness. He was her murderer. He was the dark horse that the fortune teller saw in her horoscope. She saw him killing Zelli instead of her. Yet here, in the middle of a rainy day, nothing of that mattered anymore.

Helga was losing herself willingly. Not reaching for any reason. There was the horrible, mad, exciting, clear, and flattering truth:

he killed to stop Helga from leaving him. He didn't want to be without her. Without "them." No, he would have never been able to understand that she had to leave him. That she had to break the chain of her obsession. Because, in fact, she was unable to live a day without him. One single day without seeing him, loving him, inhaling him.

He wouldn't have understood. Her whole theatre life, as she planned it, her talent she had to honor; all that would have been relinquished because, honestly, she'd rather stay in bed with him all day long. All of her days. Forever . . .

"Here! See? It was as quick as I said." He laughed the laugh that was in her ears all those years. Unchanged. Like his scent. Like the gloss of his eyes. Her life as she'd tried to build it without him had just evaporated.

Marcel's face was above her, in that perfect distance which she can always eliminate by a simple lift up on her tiptoes.

"Doing something this afternoon?"

Balancing on the tiptoes of her madness, she pulled up from the car seat to be closer to his mouth, "Making love to you, my darling."

Jacob Holzknecht picked up the telephone. It was an easy conversation. Bruno Gottliebe had a perfectly organized archive, courtesy_Miss Schlegel. Old posters, bills, notices, photographs. Jacob was there in no time.

Bruno was waiting; his head tilted to the side with a warm smile. Fatherly figure as Jacob remembered him. He gained some inches around his belt, Jacob noticed. They shook their hands warmly; Bruno spontaneously grasped Jacob's upper arm with the other hand as only a good friend would do. He still regretted that Jacob's baritone left the theatre. He could have been a good core for the male chorus. Too bad. Coffee was ready, Jacob couldn't resist. There was a sad conversation to be had.

"Aha! So that's the season we are talking about." Bruno's years ran in theatre seasons. His year started in September and ended in July.

He understood how difficult this must be for Jacob. His voice tried not to get any dark undertone when he asked, "Zelli's pictures?"

"No. It's actually the Review cast I'm interested in."

"The runaway!" Jacob stepped unwittingly on an unexploded mine. "That lousy amateur! The costume hanger! Don't remind me of her! She plowed my season left to right!"He was still very angry. "What a season! I almost didn't survive that."

Jacob was more interested in the season after he came here" You wouldn't consider lending me some of those photos, would you?" Bruno didn't hear him. He was raging with renewed energy;

"And Helga left for Berlin right after she did the show; to be with Steinhardt. She didn't even stop to say goodbye; rushed to catch her Night Express."

Jacob listened with awe. This was not how Bruno reported the whole thing. There was no word about Helga. Jacob could never forgive himself for not coming to see Zelli's debut. He didn't want to make her more nervous! Helga rushed away? That's new. He wondered why.

"Could I?"

Bruno had no interest to ever remind himself of that doom-day

"Take all you need." He bent forward over his desk" Miss Schlegel!"

The kind secretary reappeared. "Mr. Jacob I am afraid, that box you want, got discarded."

Bruno turned towards her with his whole body. "What?"

"Sorry, but you tossed that whole season, remember?"

Bruno scratched his cheek. "I did, didn't I?" He remembered his mother saying to him "Bruno, you have a fire in your butt." There, it was all gone.

Jacob finished his already cold coffee in one go and stood up. "Sorry for all that trouble, Mr. Gottlieb."

"Oh, please, didn't we drop this formality decades ago?"

Jacob laughed "Probably. So, thank you, Bruno."

"I wasn't of much help. Keep me posted."

"I will; once I'm finished with all that."

Only after Jacob left, it occurred to Bruno that he never asked him what he meant by: 'finished with all that.' *With what?*

"I thought you were in America." Marcel carefully carried a full champagne glass towards Helga's lips. White bubbles were fizzing away. She loved the foam and was after it. Her long smooth neck extended even further; her chin stretched forward; her lips embraced the edge of the fine thin glass. *Too late.* She took a long sip "I was."

"To think it took me several years to realize that I know that face under Reinhardt's imaginative make-up! Dora Glück, the star of Max Steinhardt's company. My Helga."

"You actually know of Max. You surprise me."

"I was glad. I hoped that. . ." He didn't want to say this, but she guessed anyway.

"That I changed from one theatre to the next, not from one man to the other?" Marcel's "hm . . ." was more of a breath, careful not to damage the fine balance of this moment.

"I've missed you so much, Helga."

She took the cigarette they'd been sharing into her slender pink fingers.

"But you didn't hesitate to marry." Her voice meandered up an octave in the end in an unrealized question.

"No, for you weren't there to be married." There was a potential argument. Helga chose to ignore it.

"Hmm." Smoke escaped through her delicate nose. "How true."

"Were you filming A Midsummer Night's Dream then?"

"You read film magazines?"

"My wife subscribes to them."

Helga's eyes smiled. Her head turned side to side in confirmation of her"You don't read them." She sipped more champagne. Maybe she could say this, without sounding jealous, "Max chose someone else over me to play Titania."

"No!"

"That's why I'm here, darling. I've taken some leave from all that; decided to come back home; wherever it may be."

"To Vienna?" Marcel stopped thinking. He was carried through time and tried to avoid questions about what was to come next; now he knew it all was going to be real again. They will start all over . . . Marcel rolled with new energy towards her. "I have never, in my whole life, felt as happy as I am at this very moment."

"Have you forgiven me?" She asked and couldn't stop kissing his shoulders, his neck . . . . "I had forgiven you . . . I've been carrying your vesta all these years."

"My vesta?"

Helga stopped her trail of kisses. Marcel propped himself up to his elbows. "My silver vesta?"

"Yes, the one you lost. . ." She turned on her stomach, her arm reaching for her purse left on the floor when they arrived. After a brief blind search, she pulled it up ". . . in the Maze. Here." Her palm opened up.

Marcel looked closer. "It looks like mine."

"Darling, you can tell me the truth now."

"In the Maze? We never made it down there. Remember? I never lost my vesta."

"Marcel, I . . . I saw you."

"You saw me? Where?"

She wasn't sure what they were playing here. "In the theatre." She said with more intensity than she'd have liked.

He suddenly remembered. "Oh right. Theatre. Yes. You are right. I saw you in front of the stage door. Your face looked like . . . like . . . the Scream by Munch."

"It's all in the past now . . . I don't want to think about it."

"Think about what? What's in the past?"

"My murder."

"Your murder?"

"I understood your reasons . . . I forgave you and now we are back together."

"Helga, what are you talking about? Stop. I am lost."

"Down in the Maze . . . you . . . shot me in the back."

Marcel was looking at her, his eyes narrowed by his focus. "I__what?"

"You sent me a note to come to the Maze and kiss you."

"What note?"

"The one "I have to kiss you . . .""

"I couldn't send you a note that day. Helga, listen. I was at my father's, had a flat tire, was late, I hadn't seen you until that second by the stage door."

Helga's voice started speeding up. "Just tell the truth. Tell the truth, please. I saw you. You came in so quickly. I was watching Zelli, she was sniffing cocaine!"

"Cocaine? Slow, slow down. This is maddening, please."

"I wanted to run and stop you from coming; I didn't know what to say to her, and then . . . then you arrived—shot her in the back and_ran away . . . and . . . I . . . I watched myself die."

"What are you talking about? What do you mean by 'I watched myself'?"

"She was Me! She was wearing my full costume, my wig . . . she was doing that performance in my place!"

Only now Marcel grasped the full story. "My darling girl! You thought that I. . ."

"Yes." Helga didn't care about her tears, she was crying silently. "That you came to kill me because I was leaving you."

Marcel placed one hand on the back of her neck. Helga knew this was the moment. She felt relief. Her anxiety was over. *He is going to kill me now. Be it.*

His hand slid down her spine. He lifted her gently like a crushed flower he would pick in the meadow after rain. He placed Helga back in their sheets with all of his tenderness. His kisses closed her weeping eyes. She kept crying silently, trying to stop when he laid down next to her. But she couldn't. Only with his arm under her head Helga relaxed. She began to calm down. Marcel felt the rhythm of her breathing as it started gradually slowing down. The stillness of her sleep swept him within.

The morning was overcast, but it was just what they wanted— an excuse to stay in bed . . . to make love, to eat . . . to make love . . . Marcel had no appointments until late afternoon. Did she?

"No," said Helga, "I'm here to shop for my wardrobe for the new season . . . then I'll go to Paris next week."

"Oh!" A plan occurred to Marcel. He's here for the business he's been doing for the Embassy. His schedule is flexible. "I need to be with you . . . whatever it takes."

"You are a married man now."

"Let me deal with that. I can't be without you any longer."

Not commenting on that, not elaborating in any way, Helga was only curious about today,

"Would you go shopping with me?"

"Gladly."

"It won't be strange if somebody sees us?"

"No, not in the least. I must bring something to my wife. My friend offered her a helping hand."

Helga couldn't stand the mystery much longer. "Who is she?" she asked the next day in the fashion salon. She and Marcel watched models walking for them in the newest samples.

"A wealthy gal. I've known her almost all of her life."

"Hm . . . Lucky." A pair of dresses on the short runway caught her eye. She was deciding "Elegant or stunning?"

"Both."

"You are going to buy the two?"

"Which two? I was talking about my wife."

"Oh, is she both? Lucky for you. I meant the dresses!"

He smiled at her like an accomplice.

"She would surely love something like this. She has an impeccable taste."

Helga looked straight ahead as a new model entered the floor. Wife. She will have to get used to it. Helga tried to picture what Marcel's wife could look like. It was balancing on the verge of masochism. And comedy. As if reading her thoughts Marcel added: "You would like her. She's an athletic gale, tall and slim."

The scene from Bruno's office flashed in Helga's mind; she almost burst out laughing. The Stick. . . what was her name? Adrianne! Why of course! Helga's nickname for her was perfect: "The Costume Hanger" Her face was glowing with inner giggles. A new model had arrived. Helga forgot all about Marcel's wife. Here was a new temptation. She forgot all that annoying memory from Bruno's office. This is the new season's pale blue ensemble she has to have! She stretched her arm and her experienced fingers examined the fabric. She turned towards her lover "Yes?"

Marcel smiled, "Of course, darling. Consider it done. It's yours now."

"There was a telephone call from Vienna for you, madam" the serious-looking concierge back at Dorchester handed Helga her room key.

"Here's the message from that lady . . . and also . . ." He turned towards the cubbies behind him. " . . . a letter arrived for you, Madame." He placed it on the desk with a rigid nod. He made several swift notes with his fountain pen in a large book on the desk in front of him. When Helga finished reading the message from Sybille and looked up, he's already returned to his stillness. "Thank you."

Helga picked up the letter. She found one of the round, comfortable seats right there in the lobby. She didn't bother asking for a letter opener. The mechanical pencil, with a cobalt blue enameled body, which she always carried around, did the job. Max Steinhard's opening night present. She cherished that memory.

She saw the return address. *Aha!* Helga smiled, pleased. *Max Steinhardt, The Great, listened to my plans after all!* He knew she would stop at Dorchester. She knew that if he wanted her back on one of his stages, he would make it happen.

She glanced at the letterhead and skipped forward

"As I take it, your return to Europe is a sign of your resignation. Our association therefore ends. With enduring respect, Yours . . ." et cetera.

It was all typed; not even his signature as she knew it. It was written in English—to further distance himself from her, she guessed. She was the guilty party in his eyes; he offered her a cameo in his movie; she's the one who moved first from that unexpected stalemate. Her loss. She was certain of that. But then, Max just made everything much easier for her. He had no idea how much.

"Dora? Dora who?" Sybille's teasing giggle on the other side of the telephone conversation was unmistakable "Oh, Helga! You are back in Europe! So, what do you think?"

"I hope I don't need a new stage name."

"We need your Steinhardtian fame for our humble beginnings."

So it was agreed, sealed by a clink of champagne, long distance.

Helga was moving to Vienna again, only this time as Dora Glück, one of Max Steinhardt's former stars. She was determined to help her friends put their small cabaret up on the theatre map. She poured herself more champagne and, after she hung up, lifted it with one cheer _" To Vienna!"

Helga heard her name being called over the chaos of the platform. "Here!" She raised her arm, luggage ticket in her hand. The porter was pushing the cart with her travel trunks and boxes through the crowd.

Helga looked around. The Main Station, the Franz-Josef Banhof, in Vienna, was again a different place. Sunny, hopeful, full of wonderfully cheerful sounds. For no reason, an image flashed within her memory. She recalled that young woman, the pickpocket. Helga was in a great, generous mood. She hoped that the young thief had found a better way of life that her tides had changed. She wondered what stream carried her by now.

Perhaps one like Helga's: The new beginning! She gave an unreasonably high tip to the porter and stepped in the large black box of a taxi.

Once comfortably inside she took out the envelope with Marcel's writing. There was the address of the hotel where he'd rented a suite for them.

He had an exact plan. What exhilarating fun! They will travel from one hotel to another in Vienna, trying one honeymoon suite after another. It was brilliant!

However, she rented an apartment for herself; to have her own basis, her very own home.

She didn't know how, or if to tell him at all, but then decided to go ahead.

Several hours later, at the moment when he was all dressed to leave, she found the moment to say "Darling, I'd almost forgotten. I rented an apartment."

"Why?" There was an annoyed tone.

"To have. To be my own mistress. To have my pots and pans." She was half-dressed, trying to fasten a small button in the back of her neckline. Marcel didn't offer to help. He slipped in his overcoat. Was there a sudden rush in his movements? "I have to go. We'll talk about it tomorrow."

His kiss came merely as a brush of his lips. Did the pots and pans do it?

Marcel left and Helga stopped rushing home.

She wondered if he avoided their kiss because he was already 'at home' in his mind with his 'Elegant and Stunning' wife. Married bliss or her apartment?

Several moments later the phone rang. Helga picked up but stayed silent. Marcel's voice asked "Helga?" She wasn't at her usual quick mode to answer.

"Yes."

"Don't forget, darling, we are booked here through Sunday." His voice was seductive and warm. Helga smiled; here was her answer: it was her apartment. Her smile warmed up her "I won't."

Marcel sent her a kiss.

The next morning Helga had a meeting in her friend's cabaret. It was not far from the center but as she looked around she couldn't imagine walking in this street late at night.

The conversation was harder than Helga expected. Long-distance calls remodeled the theatre already to a cabaret of Sybill's vision. The reality couldn't be worse.

"So, what do you think?"

The space was small and stank of mold and beer from the above beer cellar.

"It has a definite charm. . ." She was polite. The all-black space was for about fifty people, sitting on benches in steep bleachers.

Those on top would choke in heat. The rectangular stage in the bottom part would be overcrowded by six actors. The first row barely left space for feet between the chair and the low stage. She sat down. "Hmm . . . my face is in somebody's lap. . ." she looked at Sybille, "...and not of my own choice."

They giggled. "You haven't changed!"

"Aren't you glad?"

Sybille shrugged her bony shoulders in her cardigan. The colorful zigzag pattern made it look like a surrealist animation. "You hate it here."

"No, no," rushed Helga with a reassuring tone. "I just think a larger space might be. . ."

"We weren't able to put together more money." Sybille stood center stage and looked suddenly positively beat. Helga was overwhelmed by the smell down here. "Sybille, let's have a coffee somewhere and talk."

"No need. Without you, we won't be able to keep afloat. There."

She was right. There was the truth. Sybille was a multi-talented artist. Helga met her at a dance class soon after she arrived from Switzerland. She saw a desperate call for help. Had the circumstance "out there" offered any chance for Sybille, Helga was certain she would have picked it up. "How much?" Not waiting for her friend's answer, Helga wrote a check.

Sybille hesitantly took it. "This is a loan, right?" Only then her eyes focused on the sum. Before she could say anything Helga was rapidly walking out. "It's a gift, and we'll never talk about it again."

"Are you here, darling?" Marcel opened the bedroom door.

Gerda had just taken her afternoon bath. She was thoroughly scented, her hair under a white turban. "Hmmm." Marcel smelled her neck. "When did you say we have to be at that darn restaurant?"

Gerda giggled" It's your darn restaurant and your darn business dinner! Who is that friend of yours?"

Gerda asked from her husband's thighs. He was busy kissing her neck.

"He's . . . someone. . . I used to know in college. He's a French financier."

"Will it be only him?"

Marcel's kisses traversed soft complexion towards Gerda's mouth. "He says he might bring someone he used to know in . . . Switzerland, perhaps."

"Oh, no. Not another 'moneyman'?" Gerda stepped down on the black carpet.

"I'm afraid so, darling . . . but look on the bright side: you'll be able to practice your French!" She unwound the towel turban and shook her freshly permed hair, "I'm dying of excitement."

Marcel flew to her with several large low steps "Come here, you! We still have twenty minutes before we have to dress."

Gerda was relieved. No, there was positively no one else. She let her robe fall on the floor. In that very second, she made a mental note to herself: Stop her private detective. Cancel it all. Such a stupid idea. She was right when she told him that Marcel was hers. He is. Only hers.

The restaurant was full. This was the place to come to be seen, if you meant something, in Vienna. Everybody was here. Marcel's French friend, Simon Goldblum, insisted Marcel brought his wife. He wanted to introduce them to his old friend. Evidently, that friend was a star worth the acquaintance.

They met accidentally a few days ago after not seeing each other for ages.

"That sounds like a happy coincidence to me." Marcel was already planning his future contact with the stranger. Possibility to stir things to his own advantage had to be investigated.

A quiet restaurant, sort of a club. Perfect service. They had cocktails. Simon was very charming. He looked like a mix of Ramon Novarro and Errol Flynn; he knew it well. So did the ladies in this room. He flirted exclusively with Gerda from the moment they were introduced.

She was flattered. Marcel was amused. Gerda observed with unfailing amazement how men seemed to always pick up the vibe. The invisible trace of lovemaking, sex, and blood of the moon. The secret map of the woman's face. It seemed as if they all knew her afternoon with Marcel down to details. Simon was their envoy. His eyes didn't leave hers for too long; although it was difficult not to stare at her earrings; those were some of the largest diamonds he'd ever seen. They were fashioned after the famous pairs of cherries, worn by Russian tzarinas on their wedding day. He assumed they were her husband's wedding gift to her. Gerda told him with pride that he was correct.

He held her hand that little moment too long, which tells a woman she's desired. He'd pass her a glass of wine, lit her cigarette with the secret touch of his soft fingertips. Marcel was amused. Never jealous. This was business. He saw how much pleased Simon was and played along.

It was important to Marcel that his friend had a great time. They were about to close an exciting financial deal in the next few days.

Suddenly there was a little rush in the room. The level of sound raised like a wave, by the entrance some patrons began applauding.

Marcel turned in that direction. He stopped breathing. His wife's face lost all its glow.

In the aisle, between the two rows of tables, was Helga, coming towards Marcel. She was dressed in the same evening gown Gerda chose for tonight: The silver lamé Vionnet dress she had admired in London.

She came to their table to say Hello to Simon; she quickly summed up the situation. Her "You must excuse me; I have a previous engagement I forgot about. I just came to say Goodnight and thank you for waiting," was heard clear and wide. She didn't look at any of them. When she turned, she had no problem sharing smiles with people who recognized her from the Operetta ("that's Helga Hayden!") and some who knew her from Steinhardt ("Look . . . is that Dora Glück? Is she back in Vienna?").

Her complex exercise of self-control lasted until she arrived at her apartment.

She started laughing; in a few seconds, she felt a strange urge never to stop. She couldn't rid her mind of that vista_The frozen torso of Marcel's wife! Still, in fits of giggles she poured herself a small glass of slivovitz. Then she lifted it and against good judgment drank it on a hungry stomach_ Prosit _ the way Bruno always recommends: all in one go. There came the sway. She found her bed and as she was, in her twin silver lameé bespoke Vionnet, fell forward and slept.

Three hours later Marcel flew into her apartment. "What were you thinking?!"

Helga was just waking up; she couldn't believe Marcel's rage. "That was a sheer disaster!"

"Marcel, how could I know? I had no idea you bought it. I went back to that place and got it the next day."

Marcel sat down on the edge of her new white leather sofa. "Oh, what a night!"

Helga sat up in her bed and crossed her legs. It wasn't exactly clear what he meant by

"Great deal, by the way." and "How do you know Simon? Nevermind" and of course his "Gerda was very brave."

Helga was too tired for that. "Oh yes, that's right. She was . . . very brave." It sounded as flat as she hoped it would. Marcel had to be very tired not to hear the sarcasm.

Helga decided to forget about the whole scene. She knew she played it fair and straight. "Will I see you tomorrow?"

"I don't know yet. I think not."

"Of course. I have a stack of books and a play I want to read."

"I will call you."

"Yes, do."

"Not a serious drama, I hope?" Marcel walked carefully around her as if his tuxedo could get saturated with her scent. Helga wished it did and then started dripping in front of Gerda in their cozy art deco living room an hour later. She said under her breath" No, not yet" but he didn't catch the irony. Marcel wasn't listening anymore.

"I <u>will</u> call you." He said again as if she doubted his promise, which she did. He surely knew her well.

The next day neither of them picked up the receiver, no messages, no attempts to contact each other. Helga read books, leafed through some magazines. She never touched the play. She dressed and went to a museum; in the afternoon she stopped at a café and bought herself a full apple-strudel to take home.

She shut the world behind her, put her house keys in a ceramic bowl among dry pomegranates when she heard a man clearing his throat inside her living room. She knew that timber.

With a fragile strudel above her head as a weapon ready to strike an intruder, she kicked the door open.

The effect on her lover was as she'd hoped; Marcel gave a roar of laughter, hopped up from the armchair to embrace her. The decision on whether to make love and then eat or eat and then make love was unanimously decided and voted for both.

It certainly was a social disaster. Nothing short of a catastrophe some would say. Not for Gerda. Like other actresses, like Helga, her clothes were her costumes. No, her shock-stricken face had nothing to do with the silver lamé Vionnet.

Just like a few guests in the restaurant, Gerda immediately recognized Helga.

She almost fainted; but then, helped by her theatre experience she rapidly assumed a new role_ that of a hostess. She survived the evening; more, she took over it and flew with high marks!

She danced and entertained their French guest all evening long. Her rusty French was considered charming. She would have sworn that Simon was falling a little bit in love with her. Marcel was ecstatic; she helped him make a lot of money that night. When he sent her home and stayed behind with Simon, she was relieved. She cried in the back seat of their large, golden Isotta.

Her maid was concerned. Gerda didn't want to talk, handed her the diamonds, and sent her away.

Gerda poured sleeping pills into her palm. She could take them all at once. A full glass of water was in her hand; she started counting them.

When she woke up, the next day at noon, it was into a different life. She was a murderer of an innocent woman; a poor, nameless somebody whom she mistook for Helga_her archenemy!

Marcel left early to work. He left her a message. He slept in the guest room, it said. Must finish the deal with Simon. It was as well.

Gerda decided to stay in bed all day, citing poor health. She was having a late breakfast. Her thoughts were trying to find order. She picked up the home telephone and called down "Make me a drink, Johan." Her husband's favorite servant was a master of mixing drinks. He wasn't sure what was going on. This was an early hour for his creations, but he was here to serve: "Something light, fruity perhaps, madame?"

"I'll leave it to your taste" Gerda tried to smile. Then added "Something stronger."

How much Johan knows? That would be interesting to hear. No, he would never tell on Marcel.

Johan finished mixing her cocktail. Gerda took a sip. Johan was waiting. Elegant, gray hair slicked back; fully clad in crisp white jacket with golden epaulets of his livery.

She didn't feel like talking; but there was her discipline: "It's very good. Thank you. That will be all, Johan, I need some rest."

"Thank you, madam" Johan left without making any noise. She was grateful.

Gerda knew now, with absolute certainty, who was guilty_ it was all Helga's fault that Gerda murdered an innocent young woman!

Gerda's mind worked on excess; she didn't finish her cocktail, and instead drank a glass of freshwater. She didn't feel better, only her stomach felt full and unpleasantly heavy. She crossed to the phone and called Jacob Holzknecht and associates. "Any progress?" She listened with the utmost attention. The young associate, she recalled the bouncing curl on his forehead, gave her the newest report. Her eyes opened wider. Her mouth dried out.

"The Royal honeymoon suite?" She heard herself repeat his words. She couldn't believe she heard that correctly and made him say that again. Her composure was a result of lifelong practice. It always served her well in the end.

"Very well." Gerda finished her cocktail. "No further instructions; you'll give me the report next week." She forgot to be polite and hung up.

Jacob Holzknecht was sitting over his afternoon coffee and cake. Those past weeks he'd been thinking often of his Zelli. It was curious how memory comes in waves; enchants you, hurts you, excites you . . . then leaves you; in Jacob's case leaving a void. Deep and dark; murky like the mine in Salzburg where they tossed a coin into the deep shaft, waited, counting the seconds until they heard it splash hundreds of feet underneath. Their wish was safe, they thought.

Jacob has been waiting for something. A sound from the dark, something that would help him understand where to go look for Zelli's murderer. But it was, perhaps, too much to ask. His investigation among the notorious Viennese drug dealers led nowhere.

His housekeeper stepped in; short, her small hands, red from years of washing floors and dishes, firmly clutching an old black leather purse. She was all dressed to go home. "I will see you tomorrow at ten. If you'd have the shirts ready for me . . . Thank you."

"Thank you, Mrs. Kunz, I will see to it." She was a treasure. She left behind the scent of heavy lilac, the cheap and popular line of 'Blooms Alive' Eau de. Every bottle contained blooms macerated in alcohol; devoid of their color, the flowers looked like specimens for the anatomy class.

She put her head around again" Your associate called. He wasn't sure about something."

"Thank you. I'll ring him up later." He heard the door closing, her heels clicking on the terrazzo floor toward the elevator.

Jacob stood up. First, he should take the dishes to the kitchen. She spoils him. He'll rinse them later. He has to call his office later too. There were more important things for him to do now.

He crossed back and sat on the thin faded carpet.

The box with Zelda's theatre photographs was waiting for him. Reluctantly he took the one on top. A group of chorus girls. That was the production where they met.

Jacob wasn't certain what he was doing now. It was all just an intuition. But he learned to trust it.

He systematically divided photos by the costumes. Operetta after operetta, then the review. The first Zelli's solo. All her hopes. Jacob's anger seeped in from a long-forgotten well in his memory.

As he was looking through the black and white world, Zelda's voice was coming back to him. Gradually he began remembering what she told him. There was a new girl. It was her who inspired Bruno Gottlieb to do the review.

What was her name? But there was just a painful haze in his memory. Zelda said something about her that shocked him then. Yes. He remembers now. Zelda said that she was trying to push into Marcel's bed. She thought it didn't go anywhere. Zelli also said something else. He forgot.

Gerda parked on a diagonal from the hotel. She knew her way around. She honeymooned here with Marcel for three nights before they took off on the Orient Express. Now he is here with Helga!

She sat in the car, her head about to shatter into million splinters. She couldn't believe this. This must be an error. A frightening daydream. She will wake up and all this will be gone. But this was not a bad dream. Not even a bad joke. Too late now. She could have lived happily ever after with Marcel till the day they died . . .

There must be a service staircase from this side somewhere. She waited and watched. Until dinner ten days ago she had hope. There she suddenly understood. The way Marcel looked at the woman. Gerda recognized her right away; especially in all that glitter. It was like being on the stage again: enter Miss Helga. There are three bullets for her in Gerda's revolver. Three. She deserves them all.

There were linen maids coming out to take a quick puff. So there's the staff entrance.

Gerda opened her glove compartment. She still remembered how to attach a silencer.

Marcel ordered a lot of champagne to celebrate. This suite was called "The Royal Honeymoon Suite." He and Helga had been happy here. He extended the booking for the whole month.

The unfortunate incident in the famous restaurant was long forgotten. Women! Marcel saw the simplicity of that scene immediately; it was called: Two Ladies in the Same Dress. It was solved by his lover walking away. She has class. He couldn't be prouder of his gorgeous wife! Her self-control? Remarkable! By mid-dinner, Gerda was calm and entertaining. Brilliant. The deal with Simon went very well. That mattered. More money in the bank. Excellent! Gerda was such a good sport. Good girl. All forgotten, all forgiven.

With Helga, it was different. She's an artist, an actress; he had to cajole her, bribe her, play more to her emotions. She finally gave in. The fact that he'd honeymooned with his wife here was an added aphrodisiac for Marcel.

Their excitement was fueled by the novelty of their surroundings, by the fact that the danger was real. That they might be caught at any given time made this adventure so much more thrilling. Their secret was like a heavy, hot spice, addictive to the point that regardless of your headache you want more.

Jacob was careful with the next shoebox. It was all too personal. It hurt. Those photographs were special for Zelli. They were those with autographs, some with personal messages.

Jacob didn't rush to open it. He could still see her shocked face, her surprise . . . "How did you know?" She had been looking every week at the Italian shoemaker's shop window. Her fireworks of joy! He loved those shoes on her. *Oh, Zelli . . .*

Before he could open the shoebox, the telephone rang. It was his associate. The mandatory routine report: Marcel in the hotel with Helga, booked for a week, call with any changes. Done.

Jacob opened the lid. The time stopped then reversed.

He was taking out all the snapshots of Zelda he took himself one by one, and placed them aside. Underneath was a thick stack of photographs of all sorts. People Zelda admired, postcards of Rudolph Valentino, Pola Negri, Gloria Swanson . . . many publicity photos of her famous colleagues and guest stars, autographed. There was the 'new blond girl'. Across the bottom part of the studio shot, she wrote a simple 'To Zelli, Adrianne!' That was the girl!

Jacob walked up briskly to the dining table and took out the magnifying glass from the deep drawer. There . . . he couldn't be mistaken.

The afternoon was lazy and wonderfully long. Marcel said to Gerda he's still working on his deal. She'd never questioned anything he said. Never. Since she was a little girl, really. He was relaxed and content.

Champagne finally arrived. He heard the door open in the ante-room.

"Leave it on the table, thank you!"

The door closed. Marcel didn't want them to be bothered by the valet.

He was just explaining to Helga his new plan. She was listening to him carefully. She could be absolutely certain that he meant what he was planning. But Helga was a young woman with common sense; it told her that all of it was Marcel's fruitful fantasy.

They finished their shared cigarette, and Marcel had a plan: "Look, Gerda is a good woman, she'll understand. After all, you were with me long before she appeared . . . she tricked me into all this. She was a little girl when I knew her; after that, I hadn't seen her all my life. She will do what I. . .."

"She will do what?" Gerda certainly knew how to make her entrance.

Helga instinctively pulled the blanket over their naked bodies.

"So . . . this is your 'deal'?" Gerda's voice didn't give away any of her emotions. She stood there, elegant in her ivory trench and fashionable turban in moss green velvet. Her calm was enviable.

Both Gerda and Helga were relieved that Marcel didn't try to say something along the lines of 'This isn't what it looks like.' Instead, he said: "Go home, Gerda. I'll come soon. We'll talk."

"Talk? There's nothing to talk about. "She started taking off her gloves." No more. . . No more. Finished."

She walked up to the first low armchair in the salon and sat down. She left the bedroom door open. Gerda had her hair done at noon, right after the detective reached her. Change of hair color. She was sure Marcel would love this one.

Jacob Holzknecht lowered the magnifying glass one more time. He took a pencil and with renewed fervor quickly blackened Adrienne's hair.

He stared at the result._Adrianne, as she called herself then, turned to Baroness Van Getz.

Before Jacob could reach the phone, it rang. It was his associate again. "I forgot to tell you. I spoke to Baroness Van Getz, she wanted the full report. So I. . ."

"You what?"

Jacob dropped the receiver. It suddenly came to him what Zelda told him Adrianne said:

"I will kill them if he can't be mine."

Jacob left his hat behind and started running. He rushed out the main door yelling desperately for a taxi.

He kept running forward in the direction of the hotel.

This was now a question of time and death.

Marcel felt almost joy. *She's going to divorce me! That's what she means, right?* He would have hugged her if the situation wasn't so awkward. He crossed the bedroom and closed the door behind his wife.

Helga and Marcel dressed quickly in a silent cloud of empty thoughts. Only the noise of popped champagne from the other room, the crunch of ice cubes in the ice bucket was making an odd white noise.

They finally appeared in the doorway; Marcel went through first. He tried not to make any noise. He held the chair for Helga, then pulled one of the brocade tabourets towards the small table and sat down. Everything was so smooth and sophisticated.

"How did you . . . ?" But before he finished asking, he answered himself. "You hired a private detective."

"Yes, a private detective." Gerda nodded and took a sip of champagne.

"When did you know?"

"I didn't. I simply couldn't stop suspecting you since the beginning."

"Suspecting me?" Marcel was evidently hurt and appalled.

Gerda didn't answer, her shoulders did; they slid up and down. "I hired him a year ago or so and never dismissed him; that's all. I forgot about it. One Jacob . . . somebody . . . Holzknecht!"

Helga managed to stay silent. Her hands involuntarily grabbed the armrests.

Gerda promised herself to be civilized, not to yell, not to lose her cool.

Without saying a word Marcel poured champagne. Helga even didn't notice.

He offered to refill Gerda's glass. Her long fingers blocked the champagne coupe "No, thank you. I had enough."

Helga saw her red nails and heavy golden rings. If it was supposed to make a statement, it did. Marcel poured for himself. "To us! I suppose . . ."

Helga looked at her lover in disbelief. She didn't touch her drink.

Gerda told herself that it all has to be done with class. She wasn't one of those women who go crazy, grab a gun and . . . No, not her. She made sure that she looked her best. She dressed the part; the bright spotlight was on her. This was the soliloquy she'd never had a chance to act on stage. Now she could, center stage.

She stood up. Helga noticed how skinny she looked under her trenchcoat.

Her speech started coming slowly, evenly paced. Her voice surprised Helga, the actress, with its pleasant timber.

"Every woman will understand, have pity; every woman who ever loved will see all I had to do. . .

Helga saw it first: This was all a plan that went awry. Gerda lost. Now they will pay for it.

It was Marcel who couldn't comprehend. This woman here was the little girl, Gerda, his wife. She adores him. She couldn't harm him; what is she talking about? "Gerda, girl . . . what's this all about?"

"Every court in the world will free me." Gerda's hand slipped under the turban. Her chin down, eyes firmly hung in Marcel's, widening in disbelief.

"You still don't know, do you?" Blond tight curls exploded around Gerda's face as she freed them from the binding.

The effect was sensational. In front of them stood__"Adrianne?"

Helga noticed the gun that was suddenly in Gerda's hand. *She's skillful. No doubt.*

Looking at the elegant pampered creature, composed, ice-cold, Helga said without looking at her lover:

"She will kill us . . . she will shoot us the way she shot me . . . down in the Maze."

Gerda stopped and looked straight at Helga. Her gun pointed at her husband whose "You couldn't. . .?" made her aware of her power.

Marcel watched, paralyzed, not sure what could make this worse; he was confused, afraid to move. Then the unthinkable happened; Helga started moving toward Gerda.

"Why, Gerda? Why have you been doing all this?"

Marcel wanted to yell, to stop her. But his voice collapsed inside him. He was a helpless spectator held at point-blank by his wife. Where was the hero, he thought he had inside him?

Helga stopped. Gerda's hands stopped trembling. She hasn't stopped pointing at Marcel but brought her hands together, and unlocked the gun. "Because he's mine . . ." Her face was sweating very lightly, only to the point of gloss. She started looking like a porcelain doll. ". . . because Marcel belongs to me."

She pointed the gun at Helga's face. This was Marcel's chance.

"Because it was always you. You. You don't even know where we met first, do you?"

Marcel's fear turned to panic. Marcel turned to an observer.

"I was just a little, ugly, plump girl of no importance to you . . . Miss Helli! Helena, the Beautiful, who knows everything, who's first in everything; Helena who gets there first, gets the leading parts in all of our school plays."

Helga exhaled. "The boarding school."

"See? You didn't even know I existed!" Her voice started picking up speed. "And when I entered a completely new world to be with Marcel—there you were again! You got there first! You were on his arm, in his bed; and I was just nothing! Just the little Gerda again. 'Little girl, go out to play!' No!" She screamed and stomped her foot. Marcel had no concept of what he could do. His wife moved closer to his lover. "That was supposed to end in the Maze! What was that stupid girl doing there? I killed an innocent girl because of you! An innocent silly girl! And then. . . I had to get rid of that. . . that shabby woman."

Marcel was aghast. His voice made a pitiful comeback, "What do you mean get rid of?"

"I had to!" Gerda started sobbing. "She. . . she blackmailed me."

"Blackmail? Oh, Gerda, my poor girl. What have you done!" Marcel's body moved forward.

Gerda pointed at him; she didn't stop sobbing "I'll shoot you, darling, don't you think for one moment that I will save my precious Marcel. You wait your turn! I just want to see the two of you together frightened out of your wits!"

Gerda's voice dropped down to deep tones of hate. Her eyes were clawing Helga's face" You . . . you took the most precious. . . I lost . . . because of you . . . I lost our baby" Her words disintegrated, her sobs became blade sharp noises of deep sorrow. Helga saw a devastated young woman and felt pity.

But Marcel was looking at the woman who carries his family name, and here, in public exhibiting a mad display of her emotions, "Gerda! Control yourself! You are my wife! You are Van Getz! Stop this childish nonsense! You stop it! Now!"

There was a second of absolute silence. Helga couldn't believe what he just said. She has never met this Marcel before.

But Gerda knew him well. The look on her face was that of a little girl. Helga saw it. Gerda's last sobs rising in her chest shook her voice as she exhaled.

She pointed the barrel back at Helga. Her adult face was now composed.

They stood so close to each other it didn't matter whom she'd shoot first. She was done with them. There was one more thing to say."You decided for me. Remember?" Gerda started pointing from one to the other in a mad torturous 'cat-and-mouse' play. She was swaying in the rhythm of that new game.

"In front of my mother, you said, 'you are the future Baroness Van Getz.'" Gerda laughed through her tears. "Baroness Marcel Van Getz. And__here I am! And always will be; and no one, you hear me? No One will take my place!" She took one step back."On your knees!"

They didn't move. Gerda's anger reached a higher level "On your knees!"

Her brain made one step aside. To the place, she'd forgotten.

"Pray!"

The shot rang loud. Helga's shoulders closed over her ribcage; her head dropped down on her chest. Marcel jumped forward to catch her, fainting, in his arms.

Gerda's body collapsed on her knees and folded down to the blue carpet.

Jacob's hollow voice, still in the doorway, said to the dead silence "She murdered my Zelli, you know."

"We know," exhaled Helga, looking at Gerda's dead body.

He gave them a puzzled look, but this was all too fresh, his thoughts still unclear.

Then there was the order to follow. "I will call the police."

"Yes, of course."

Marcel, in shock, petrified, was holding his lover until she whispered, "Do we have any more champagne left?"

She wanted to cry but there were merely weak waves suggesting sobs which died out before they could reach her lips. They brought her nothing but weakness in limbs, no relief, no tears.

"We'll need something much stronger, darling." Marcel started to reemerge.

"Yes." She knew he was right. She held tightly to his waist; her hands clenched together. They were one, again. They didn't move until the police arrived.

Gerda, Baroness Van Getz, was dead.

EPILOGUE

M arcel took Helga's arm. She comfortably leaned against him with her whole body. He loved that about her. He inhaled her presence. *A new perfume?* Heavy gray silks with trims of rusty mink bounced around her ankles and her wrists. Evenings turned a bit colder these last couple of days.

They didn't go far. Their favorite Winestube, the Golden Goose, was just around the corner. The maître d ' knew them well.

This was their last night. It was better this way. She didn't ask him whether he'd like her to wave goodbye at the aero-port. South American banks were waiting for him. Her theatre was here.

They sat next to each other at the bar, sipping from two different drinks. There were no more things between them to share. Helga was turning the stem of her cocktail glass back and forth in her bare fingers. Marcel noticed a new ring. He didn't care to comment. The restaurant was reflected in the full-length mirrors behind the bar. They could safely hold onto that distant world.

He took a short gulp from his whisky on the rocks, "She had three bullets in that revolver, you know."

Helga promised herself to be generous tonight if he goes down the recent memory path. It just got harder.

"I know, Jacob told me." She lifted the short veil attached to her small Italian hat and took a long sip. *Does he really think that Gerda would have killed herself?* She kept the veil across the top of her forehead: a striking gleam of marina blue under the red mink.

This evening was a courtesy they both felt they should offer to each other. Helga had no taste for her cocktail tonight. She pushed the glass away. She couldn't think of anything harmless to say. Her small dark blue suede purse was on the bar countertop prepared to be picked up.

Helga reached for it, scooped the elegant accessory in her hands and opened it. The little mirror inside reflected her pout. The French lipstick, in Hibiscus red, fixed the imperfections. Helga was ready to go. She wrapped the mink trimmed cape around her shoulders and slipped from the bar chair.

Marcel pulled her unfinished drink towards him. "She was a great actress, after all. You must admit."

Helga Hayden, the famous European actress, turned and, without looking at Marcel, walked briskly towards the exit.

CPSIA information can be obtained
at www.ICGtesting.com
Printed in the USA
LVHW012202151121
703363LV00003B/381

9 781956 696349